A SPECIAL REPORT

Scholarship Assessed

EVALUATION OF THE PROFESSORIATE

CHARLES E. GLASSICK, MARY TAYLOR HUBER, AND GENE I. MAEROFF

AN ERNEST L. BOYER PROJECT OF
THE CARNEGIE FOUNDATION
FOR THE ADVANCEMENT OF TEACHING

JOSSEY-BASS
A Wiley Company
San Francisco

Published by Jossey-Bass
A Wiley Imprint
989 Market Street, San Francisco, CA 94103-1741   www.josseybass.com

Jossey-Bass books and products are available through most bookstores. To contact Jossey-Bass directly, call (888) 378-2537, fax to (800) 605-2665, or visit our website at www.josseybass.com.

Substantial discounts on bulk quantities of Jossey-Bass books are available to corporations, professional associations, and other organizations. For details and discount information, contact the special sales department at Jossey-Bass.

Jossey-Bass books and products are available through most bookstores. To contact Jossey-Bass directly call our Customer Care Department within the U.S. at (800) 956-7739, outside the U.S. at (317) 572-3986 or fax (317) 572-4002.

Jossey-Bass also publishes its books in a variety of electronic formats. Some content that appears in print may not be available in electronic books.

Library of Congress Cataloging-in-Publication Data

Glassick, Charles E., date.
    Scholarship assessed : evaluation of the professoriate / Charles E.
Glassick, Mary Taylor Huber, and Gene I. Maeroff ; prologue by
Ernest L. Boyer.—1st ed.
      p. cm. — (A Special report)
    Includes index.
    ISBN 0-7879-1091-0 (acid-free paper)
    1. College teaching—United States. 2. College teaching—United
States—Evaluation. 3. Learning and scholarship—United States.
I. Huber, Mary Taylor, date. II. Maeroff, Gene I. III. Title. IV. Series:
Special report (Carnegie Foundation for the Advancement of Teaching)
LB2331.G63 1996
378.1'25—dc21
                                                97-4849

FIRST EDITION
PB Printing   10 9 8 7

CONTENTS

PREFACE

ERNEST L. BOYER WAS PRESIDENT of The Carnegie Foundation for the Advancement of Teaching from 1979 until his death in December 1995. It was he who saw the need for this study, commissioned the research and writing, and presented its early results to the public. His goal was to propose standards to guide the documentation and evaluation of faculty scholarship. Working with colleagues to learn as fully as possible about current practice, Boyer developed the conceptual framework that we have enriched and expanded here. Just a month before he passed away, Ernest Boyer also wrote the prologue to this report.

A keen judge of ideas and a connoisseur of words, Ernest Boyer would rewrite a draft prepared by colleagues a hundred times, shaping it to reflect his own vision and tuning the argument to speak in his own voice. Reading aloud as he revised, Boyer could conjure up language that sounded as wonderful as it read. To our deepest regret, he did not live long enough to perform his magic on this text, and we cannot attribute it to his pen. We honor his unique contribution, however, by designating *Scholarship Assessed: Evaluation of the Professoriate* "an Ernest L. Boyer project of The Carnegie Foundation."

Designed to stand on its own, *Scholarship Assessed* is also the culmination of a larger body of work. One of the top priorities of The Carnegie Foundation during Ernest Boyer's tenure was to strengthen undergraduate education. In a series of publications, Boyer and his colleagues tried to clarify the purposes of higher education, explore what constitutes quality, and examine critically the functions that have come to be associated with the nation's colleges and universities.

For over a century, the stated mission of American higher education has been to provide teaching, research, and service. In most instances, the three purposes have been listed with the implication of equal importance. Although the balance has never been comfortable, a reasonable relationship was maintained even in the most prestigious universities throughout the first half of the twentieth century. After the Second World War, however, the balance shifted, with greatly increased emphasis on research. Teaching became less well rewarded, and service—which had been once a proud tradition of extending knowledge beyond the campus—came to mean little more than being a good citizen, lending a hand when committee work needed to be done.

The educational consequences of the new hierarchy of academic tasks have been mixed. Inquiry through specialized research has yielded marvels in all fields of study, energized top professors and their students, and kept many departments intellectually alive. But, as we at The Carnegie Foundation have argued in several recent books, the skewing of the mission of higher education toward research has also created a crisis of purpose in American colleges and universities. As other important academic functions have become undervalued, the costs to undergraduate education have been especially high.

First, the forces pushing faculty to become ever more narrowly committed to their core disciplines have contributed significantly to the weakening of general education for undergraduates. In *A Quest for Common Learning* (1981), Ernest Boyer and Arthur Levine asked whether it was possible to close the gap between the rhetoric and the reality of the curriculum; they argued that higher priority must be given to making connections, to understanding the world in the round. General education has much improved since they wrote, of course, and disciplinary boundaries have blurred. But scholars who choose to attempt works of synthesis, explore interdisciplinary territory, or speak to nonspecialists are still at a disadvantage.

Second, sharing knowledge through teaching, though expected of virtually all faculty, has suffered greatly in prestige as specialized research came to be viewed as the only form of scholarship worthy of the name. As Burton Clark noted in *The Academic Life,* published by The Carnegie Foundation in 1987, "The greatest paradox of academic work in modern America is that most professors teach most of the time, and large proportions of them teach all the time, but teaching is not the activity most rewarded by the academic profession nor most valued by the system at large."[1]

When professional priorities do not include teaching, advising, and building relationships with students, the intellectual and social environment of the college or university is weakened. *College: The Undergraduate Experience in America,* also published in 1987, advised students and their families seeking a good college to ask the following fundamental questions about faculty: "At research insti-

tutions, is good teaching valued as well as research, and is it an important criterion for tenure and promotion? Is superior teaching rewarded through recognized
status and salary incentives? Do other institutions have a flexible policy, recognizing that some faculty are great teachers, others great researchers, and still others offer a blend of both? Are *all* professors, even those who are not publishing
researchers, encouraged to be *scholars*, remaining on top of their discipline?"[2]

The application of knowledge through professional service is the third function that has suffered from too narrow a definition of scholarship. Service no
longer conjures up the image of the scholar in shirtsleeves, meeting the intellectual challenge of using the most advanced knowledge to address complex
social and technical problems. Today service has become equated with committee work on campus or in professional associations, or volunteer work in the
community. The 1990 report *Scholarship Reconsidered: Priorities of the Professoriate* argued that the application of knowledge should be understood as an
act of scholarship on a par with the discovery of knowledge through research,
the integration of knowledge, and the sharing of knowledge through teaching.

The goal of *Scholarship Reconsidered* was, in fact, to move beyond the "teaching versus research" debate and give scholarship a broader, more efficacious
meaning. The challenge was to define the work of faculty in ways that enrich,
rather than restrict, the quality of undergraduate education. Indeed, *Campus
Life,* another 1990 report, argued that a college or university should be, first of
all, "an educationally purposeful community, a place where faculty and students share academic goals and work together to strengthen teaching and learning."[3] Without a better balance among professional priorities, gaps will widen
between fields of knowledge, between faculty and students, and between campus and the larger society. Members of the community of scholars will drift far-
ther apart.

Scholarship Assessed continues this line of thought. The academy must con-
front the central question of evaluation, or it will not be able to renew the vitality of college learning because scholarship will remain too narrowly defined.
Academics feel relatively confident about their ability to assess specialized
research, but they are less certain about what qualities to look for in other kinds
of scholarship, and how to document and reward that work. Is it possible to
develop criteria and procedures for assessing the scholarship of integration,
application, and teaching that would have credibility not only across the departments on each individual campus but across campus lines as well?

Research Considerations

In preparation for this report, we have studied the literature, consulted faculty
handbooks and policy statements from scores of institutions, hosted and
attended conferences on the subject, and conducted several small surveys of

our own. In 1992, for example, we asked university presses, scholarly journals, and granting agencies about the criteria they ask reviewers to use in evaluating manuscripts and proposals. We also solicited information about faculty evaluation from more than six hundred universities. In 1994, we conducted a formal survey of all the four-year colleges and universities in the United States on the reexamination of faculty roles and rewards.

Higher education is a moving target. Facts painstakingly gathered are quickly outdated, especially today as the climate for colleges and universities rapidly changes. Presses, journals, and granting agencies may already have revised the specific criteria they use to judge manuscripts and proposals since we inquired. Campuses may have added new language to their guidelines for faculty evaluation.

Readers should also be aware that in higher education the terms of employment are in flux. In our references to "tenure" throughout this report, we have in mind any kind of contractual arrangement for continuing faculty employment. Whatever the provision for long-term positions, we assume that they will involve an evaluation of scholarly work. Similarly, academic careers will continue to evolve, and *Scholarship Assessed* should help identify paths for faculty growth and development.

Acknowledgments

No study of this scale could have been undertaken without the help of many dedicated and talented people. First and foremost, we wish to acknowledge the signal contributions of Ernest Lynton. In 1992, at Ernest Boyer's request, Lynton prepared a detailed discussion of scholarly work. Over the course of that spring and summer, the two "Ernies" and Mary Huber met regularly to explore the issues involved—a collaboration that continued in various forms throughout the years. Ernest Lynton's writing has provided a rich vein of ideas and examples that we have returned to again and again in our later work. A generous colleague, he has kept us thinking about such basic questions as what makes work scholarly, and how different types of scholarship interrelate. Because discovery, integration, application, and teaching are interrelated, they share qualities and characteristics that permit a common framework to guide faculty assessment.

From the beginning, we have also enjoyed wise counsel and warm support from Russell Edgerton and his colleagues at the American Association of Higher Education. During these years, the AAHE was exploring critical issues in faculty evaluation through its Teaching Initiative, led by Patricia Hutchings; its support of Lynton's work on professional service; and most particularly through its Forum on Faculty Roles and Rewards, led first by Clara Lovett and then by Eugene Rice. The forum's conferences, held annually since 1993, have inspired and informed us, providing entrée to a wide range of scholars and practitioners concerned with the condition of scholarly work in colleges and universities today. Indeed, it was at the 1994 conference that Ernest Boyer first presented the outline of *Scholarship Assessed,* and at the 1997 conference that Charles Glassick announced the study's completion.

Several scholars helped give direction to this report. Anne Draffkorn Kilmer sparked interest in the ancient history of the word *scholar.* Warren Bryan Martin contributed ideas about the meaning of scholarly community and kept us sensitive to philosophical issues that have divided the academy in recent years. The overriding importance of trust in the process of faculty evaluation was emphasized by Ernest Boyer's brother, University of Wisconsin historian Paul Boyer. Paul Burgess pointed out the importance of rewarding faculty for their contribution to fulfilling an institution's mission, rather than according to their value in the academic marketplace. Robert Diamond shared with us early results of his work with the disciplinary and professional associations on the definition of scholarship, as well as his surveys of faculty and deans on the relative importance of research and undergraduate teaching.

We would also like to acknowledge the timely contribution of participants at a conference held in Princeton in March 1993. At this seminar, a Carnegie Foundation team had the opportunity to develop ideas for *Scholarship Assessed* in conversation with Paula Brownlee and Russell Edgerton from higher education associations; Robert Blackey, Milton Blood, Phyllis Franklin, Samuel Hope, Carla Howery, and Ivan Legg from disciplinary and professional associations; and Paul Burgess, Carol Cartwright, Robert Diamond, Philip Dubois, Susan Forman, Mark Lapping, Clara Lovett, and Calvin Moore from colleges and universities.

Many good colleagues helped trace the contours of current practice in the evaluation of scholarship. In particular, we thank Mary Jean Whitelaw, director of data management at The Carnegie Foundation. She helped design and conduct our campus surveys, as well as our inquiries to university presses, scholarly journals, and granting agencies. She also prepared and checked the tables and appendices presenting the results of our 1994 Survey on Faculty Roles and Rewards. For assistance on formulating survey questions, we are grateful to Russell Edgerton, Myron Henry, Robert Hochstein, Patricia Hutchings, Ernest Lynton, Clara Lovett, Warren Bryan Martin, Lee Mitgang, and Eugene Rice. We owe thanks to Craig Wacker for data entry.

Hundreds of campus officials took the time to respond to our survey and send us faculty guides, committee reports, and instruments for the student evaluation of teaching. At The Carnegie Foundation, Sarah White, Michelle Light, Amy Strano, and Meredith Unruh brought order to this wealth of material and found many of the examples of good practice that we cite in this report. We learned, too, from visits of college and university administrators and faculty to our office in Princeton. In particular, we acknowledge the metropolitan university provosts, led by Joel Anderson, who joined us in August 1995; representatives from The

Associated New American Colleges, led by Jerry Berberet, who visited in October 1995; and the distinguished group of scholars and university administrators from Sweden, Australia, and the United States that convened in October 1996.

The Carnegie Foundation staff have helped tremendously. Hinda Greenberg kept a world of information at our fingertips, educated us about technical literature on peer review systems, and assembled a fascinating collection of quotations on the themes of scholar and scholarship. Jan Hempel wrote a valuable paper on portfolio approaches to documenting teaching, in addition to her sensitive editorial work on the text. Jack Osander helped explore the history of faculty evaluation. Carol Tate and Johanna Wilson gave invaluable aid in organizing and tracking down citations and references, obtaining permissions, and in keeping our quotations precise.

Special thanks are due the colleagues who read this manuscript as it was taking final shape. Carol Cartwright, Robert Hochstein, Robert Kaplan, Ernest Lynton, Lee Mitgang, and Michael Timpane provided insightful comments, astute criticism, and thoughtful suggestions that have made this a much better book.

Several other people must be given recognition. Dawn Berberian's artistry in word processing and document design made our drafts look like published pages. Jeanine Natriello and Arlene Hobson Gundrum planned and coordinated our international seminar on "Faculty Priorities for a New Century." Laura Bell helped prepare preliminary drafts of this report for circulation and Lois Harwood produced beautiful transparencies for presentations. Louise Underwood, Rosemary Seemon, Carol Duryea, and Robert Lucas kept us all coordinated, organized, and reasonably sane.

Finally, we acknowledge our debt to *Scholarship Reconsidered.* We include in *Scholarship Assessed* a reprise of that book's history of faculty roles in American colleges and universities and a review of the new paradigm of scholarship that Ernest Boyer proposed.

In completing *Scholarship Assessed,* we have been mindful of our great loss. We will never know what this monograph would have looked like had Ernest Boyer lived. However, we do know that he hoped *Scholarship Assessed* would contribute usefully to discussion of the issues it addresses. If this book helps in shaping debates on faculty evaluation in American higher education, the goal will have been achieved.

Princeton, New Jersey
June 1997

Charles E. Glassick
Mary Taylor Huber
Gene I. Maeroff

THE AUTHORS

Charles E. Glassick, interim president of The Carnegie Foundation for the Advancement of Teaching from January 1996 to July 1997, has spoken extensively at colleges and universities in the United States and abroad on the subject of faculty evaluation. Previously, he served as president of the Robert W. Woodruff Arts Center in Atlanta, Georgia, and as the eleventh president of Gettysburg College, a position he held from 1977 to 1989.

Mary Taylor Huber is a senior scholar at The Carnegie Foundation, where she has been on the staff since 1985. A contributor to many Foundation reports and projects, she has also taught courses in public policy and anthropology at Princeton University. She is coauthor of *The Knowledge Industry in the United States: 1960–1980* and author of several books and articles on colonial society in Papua New Guinea.

Gene I. Maeroff was a senior fellow at The Carnegie Foundation from 1986 until 1997, when he became director of the Hechinger Institute on Education and the Media at Teachers College, Columbia University. He is the author of six previous books on education and the forthcoming *Altered Destinies: Making Life Better for Needy Schoolchildren.*

PROLOGUE:
SCHOLARSHIP—A PERSONAL JOURNEY

THIS STUDY ACTUALLY BEGAN in the 1980s as we at The Carnegie Foundation were completing the report *College: The Undergraduate Experience in America*. In that book, we urged campuses to be more attentive to undergraduates and to reward faculty who devoted professional time to students, both as counselors and teachers. But we knew that this reordering of priorities would not be accomplished if the faculty reward system were too narrowly restricted. In *College*, we also urged that the scope of scholarship be broadened to include the full range of academic work, with special emphasis on teaching. We said, "While not all professors are likely to publish with regularity, they, nonetheless, should be first-rate scholars." And students, when they choose a college, should ask: "Are *all* professors, even those who are not publishing researchers, encouraged to be *scholars?*"

But in a larger sense, *Scholarship Assessed* marks the end of a journey that began when I had just completed a doctoral program in the traditional research model. This led quickly to the expected, even required, publications in the specialized field of medical audiology, including an article on "Vein Plug Stapedioplasty," coauthored with a distinguished otolaryngologist at the University of Iowa Hospital, where I held a postdoctoral fellowship. Scholarship meant research and publication. As a young academic, I was committed to play by the rules since the advancement of knowledge was, for me, both intellectually and socially compelling.

But then, almost without warning, I found myself at a small liberal arts college in California. There were, I discovered, no courses in the curriculum related

1

to my specialty. Further, as academic dean, I was suddenly being asked to think not just about a single discipline but about the overall purpose of the undergraduate experience. "What are, in fact, the goals of general education?" I asked at my first curriculum meeting. "And just what do we expect students to know and be able to do when they are handed a diploma?" Slowly, it began to occur to me that scholarship required not just specialization but *integration*, too. In response to that vision of intellectual life, we organized at Upland College what was perhaps the first 4–1–4 calendar in the nation—with a January term, a time when everyone came together to explore a single theme and discover ways the separate disciplines might relate more authentically to each other.

Then, in the early 1960s, I moved to the University of California, Santa Barbara, as director of the Center for Coordinated Education, and my thoughts about the work of the academy took yet another turn. The nation was caught up in the anxiety of the post-Sputnik era. Everyone felt the urgent need to improve the nation's schools. And the goal of the Santa Barbara Center was to relate the work of the university more directly to surrounding schools. I slowly began to understand that scholarship involved not only the discovery and integration of knowledge but also the application of knowledge. We discussed constantly how the university could help close the gap between theory and practice, to be more fully engaged in pressing issues beyond the campus.

Later, I moved east and while chancellor of the State University of New York, with sixty-four campuses, I confronted, almost daily, scholarship in all its forms. We had undergraduate programs, research centers, interdisciplinary institutes, and medical schools, where the work of the academy was continuously applied.

Unexpectedly, I received a call one day inviting me to become the U.S. Commissioner of Education. In this position, I found myself looking at the full range of teaching and learning, from preschool to graduate education. I realized, as I had not done before, that education is a seamless web, and that if we hope to have centers of excellence in research, we must have excellence in the classroom. It is the scholarship of teaching that keeps the flame of scholarship alive.

At The Carnegie Foundation, after completing *College*, I began to reflect on how to define the meaning of scholarship as I had experienced its various forms over the years—as a graduate student, academic dean, chancellor, and commissioner of education. Eventually, these thoughts led to the publication of a report entitled *Scholarship Reconsidered*, in which I suggested that the work of the intellectual life included not only the *scholarship of discovering knowledge* but also the *scholarship of integrating knowledge*, the *scholarship of applying knowledge*, and the *scholarship of teaching*.

Frankly, I was surprised by the response to *Scholarship Reconsidered*. The report quickly became, for The Carnegie Foundation, a bestseller. We could barely keep the book in stock, and my colleagues and I were invited to dozens of campuses from coast to coast to discuss this new paradigm of scholarship.

We encountered, on almost every campus, an open and constructive discussion of the role of the professoriate. And in fact, the majority of campuses in America have, during the last several years, revised or begun the process of revising their standards for tenure and promotion.

Still, there was one issue that clearly called out for attention. During campus visits, I frequently heard faculty say, "The scope of scholarship should, I feel, be expanded, but the real problem we face is assessment. Just how are we to evaluate teaching, for example, and how can we be sure that standards of excellence will be protected?" That caused me to reflect, once again, on my own experience. I vividly recalled that at the end of my first teaching assignment forty years ago, the dean called me in and handed me a list of ten items on which the students had evaluated me on a six-point scale. I hadn't known that I would be assessed, much less been given any hint about what yardstick would be used. Later, while teaching students at Princeton University's Woodrow Wilson School for Public and International Affairs, a much more sophisticated evaluation form was used, but even here the students and I had little opportunity in advance to reflect on the criteria of good teaching.

I then thought about those occasions when I was on the other side of the table. As chancellor of the State University of New York, I was asked to hear appeal cases. I discovered that the standards for faculty evaluation varied dramatically from one campus to another.

Clearly, any consideration of the work of the professoriate must include both a careful consideration of the scope of scholarship and an equally careful examination of how scholarship should be assessed; that is what this report is all about. Our goal is to consider standards that might be used in assessing scholarship in all its forms.

My own personal hope for this Carnegie report is that it will contribute to the current constructive debate about the role of the professoriate, and that from such discourse common language will begin to emerge within the academy about the meaning of scholarship and how it might be authentically assessed. Above all, it is my hope that the full scope of scholarship that I observed throughout the years will be truly embraced and that the nation's colleges and universities will give new dignity and new status to the full range of intellectual life.

Princeton, New Jersey   Ernest L. Boyer
November 7, 1995

CHAPTER ONE

Scholarship in Transition

I N 1990, THE CARNEGIE FOUNDATION published the report *Scholarship Reconsidered: Priorities of the Professoriate,* which offered a new paradigm for recognizing the full range of scholarly activity by college and university faculty.
Since then, campuses across the country have been reexamining traditional ideas
about scholarship against the new, more inclusive vision we proposed—one that
goes beyond research or, as we prefer to call it, the scholarship of discovery, to
encourage scholarship in teaching, integration, and application as well.

It has become clear, however, that an essential piece is missing. The effort to
broaden the meaning of scholarship simply cannot succeed until the academy
has clear standards for evaluating this wider range of scholarly work. After all,
administrators and professors accord full academic value only to work they can
confidently judge.

At The Carnegie Foundation, we are convinced that it is indeed possible to
find standards that can be applied to each kind of scholarly work, that can orga-
nize the documentation of scholarly accomplishments, and that can also guide
a trustworthy process of faculty evaluation. But before introducing these standards and exploring their uses, let us first consider what is at stake: the capacity of higher education to meet its responsibilities for teaching, research, and
service to society.

Today's constructive and vigorous discussion about faculty roles comes at a
critical time, finding America in the midst of a major transition that continues to
challenge colleges and universities. The extraordinary growth of the post-World

War II era has ended, and what seems to matter most in this climate of constraint is doing more with less.

Meanwhile, an explosion in communications technology is changing the way information is managed and shared. Lifelong learning is increasingly important to the nation's knowledge-based economy. And college campuses, like the larger society, have grown more diverse and divided in terms of political, philosophical, and value perspectives. Policy makers, legislators, and the media increasingly view higher education not as an investment in the collective public good but as a private benefit to individuals. Thus, the goals and procedures of educational institutions and even the nature of knowledge itself have become objects of challenge and change. Assumptions that guided the academy for the last half-century no longer necessarily hold, underscoring a need to clarify campus missions and to relate the work of the faculty more directly to the realities of contemporary life.

These trends have implications for the meaning of scholarship and for the future of higher education itself. The larger issues go beyond questions of faculty promotion and tenure; they pertain to the kinds of scholarship that matter and how scholars carry out their work. In the late 1950s, shortly after Sputnik extended the Cold War to space, sociologist Robert Merton argued that America's capacity to respond to the Soviets depended on the nation's ability to encourage scientific development by recognizing excellence in research.[1] As colleges and universities today seek to bolster not only research but also teaching, integrative work, and the application of knowledge, the issue of faculty excellence that Merton raised must be addressed again so that a wider range of faculty talents may flourish.

The Traditional Mission

The history of American colleges and universities is inextricably bound to the intellectual and cultural heritage of the nation itself. The commitment to teaching reflects a collegiate tradition brought to colonial America from England. The goal was to shape the character of young students in the hope of extending the Old World's view of civilization to the New World. Teaching was, historically, the central, even sacred, function of the faculty. In 1869, more than two hundred years after the founding of Harvard, its president, Charles Eliot, could still declare that "The prime business of American professors . . . must be regular and assiduous class teaching."[2]

During the nineteenth century, however, higher learning began to shift its mission so as not only to shape young lives but also to serve a burgeoning nation. The founding of Rensselaer Polytechnic Institute in 1824 demonstrated, according to historian Frederick Rudolph, that colleges could provide "railroad-builders, bridge-builders, builders of all kinds. . . ."[3] After the Civil War, the Morrill Act established land-grant colleges to link higher learning to America's rapid agricultural and technological growth. As recently as the beginning of the twentieth century, David Starr Jordan, president of Stanford University, stated that the entire university movement in this country was "toward reality and practicality."[4] Higher education's mission of teaching was joined by a mission of service beyond the campus gate.

Another part of the mission emerged from the prestigious European tradition brought to these shores by American scholars who had pursued advanced studies in the great German universities. The Johns Hopkins University, founded in 1876, sought to emulate that tradition in its attention to doctoral studies and research, although most of the nation's colleges continued to emphasize the teaching of undergraduates. The "work of investigation," as it was called by William Rainey Harper, the founding president of the University of Chicago, added to the prevailing ideas of scholarship.[5] This approach to the discovery of knowledge spread ultimately from the biological and physical sciences to the humanities and to the incipient social sciences. By today's standards, however, expenditures for research accounted for a relatively small portion of the budget.

Not until after the Second World War, in fact, did science successfully identify itself with the national interest and get funded accordingly. Research as a model for faculty work then began to spread exponentially and to colonize the academy as a whole, aided by the creation of the National Science Foundation in 1950. During that decade, growing numbers of Ph.D. recipients from a core of influential institutions committed themselves to research and fanned out to accept appointments in departments of colleges and universities across the country. No matter how remote the destinations of these novice academicians, they remained oriented to the academic centers where they had studied, which had the effect of lessening loyalties to the institutions where they taught. In this period, historian Clara Lovett observed, "faculty came to see themselves, and to be perceived by others, as mobile, independent specialists who were members of a national talent pool."[6] It was at this time that colleges and universities of all kinds began giving their highest rewards to the small number of scholars on each campus whose research earned outside funding and prestige.

Thus began a subtle but pervasive transformation of faculty priorities in American higher education. Virtually all institutions maintained a formal commitment to undergraduate education, and teaching remained central to the culture of many liberal arts colleges. Still, institutions seeking a national reputation gained it primarily through the research accomplishments of their faculty, and young professors seeking status and mobility found it more rewarding—in a quite literal sense—to deliver papers at national meetings than to teach undergraduates. Promotion and tenure came more and more to depend on research and publication; salaries followed suit. Data from the 1987–88 National Survey of Postsecondary Faculty indicated, according to James Fairweather, that teaching at all types of institutions was "at best a neutral influence and, at worst, a negative influence on faculty income."[7] Fairweather's study showed that "even schools traditionally structured for teaching—liberal arts and comprehensive institutions—now follow the research model."[8]

The priorities of American higher education have been significantly realigned since World War II. The emphasis on graduate education and research has cast a long shadow over undergraduate education at many large universities. The prime focus at these institutions moved from student to professor, from the general to the specialized, and from loyalty to campus to fealty to profession. Colleges and universities followed what David Riesman called a "snake-like procession" as one institution after another, especially those aspiring to higher prestige, pursued the same path.[9] As the research model came to prevail, faculty members were too seldom recognized for their expertise in teaching or in applying knowledge in the service of society.

Ironically, the culture of the professoriate grew more restrictive and hierarchical at the very time that America's higher education institutions became more open and inclusive in admitting undergraduates. The academy, in other words, began to undervalue teaching just as the changing profile of the student body made the need for good teaching both more important and more challenging. Professors downplayed matters of curriculum and pedagogy to respond to a reward system that stressed research and publication.

The academy also gave short shrift to the application of knowledge, despite the country's increasing need for expert advice to cope with growing social, economic, technological, and environmental problems. Many colleges and universities have been loath to bestow academic rewards on faculty members who concentrate on applying knowledge instead of discovering it. Such resistance to an enlarged vision of faculty work limits the services that college and university faculty provide by means of outreach and extension activities.

We believe institutions of higher education that fail to recognize the need for good teaching and for engagement in society are falling out of step with the expectations of parents, students, politicians, and the larger public, as well as with their own stated goals. Indeed, we hope that the voices now questioning the reward system will soon rise to a crescendo to argue for a better way of setting expectations for faculty.

Scholarship Reconsidered

Some of the best articulated questions in the academy today on faculty roles and rewards have been inspired by The Carnegie Foundation's 1990 report, *Scholarship Reconsidered,* one of the first publications to propose that colleges and universities should make fundamental changes in order to tap the full range of faculty talent. *Scholarship Reconsidered* proposed that America's colleges and universities need a fresher, more capacious vision of scholarship. We concluded in that report that institutions should broaden the scope of scholarship, and we set out a new paradigm that views scholarship as having four separate but overlapping dimensions: the scholarship of discovery, the scholarship of integration, the scholarship of application, and the scholarship of teaching.

The first and most familiar element in this model—the scholarship of discovery—comes closest to what academics mean when they speak of research, although we intend that this type of scholarship also include the creative work of faculty in the literary, visual, and performing arts. The academy holds no tenet in higher regard than the pursuit of knowledge for its own sake, a fierce determination to give free rein to fair and honest inquiry, wherever it may lead. At its best, the scholarship of discovery contributes not only to the stock of human knowledge but also to the intellectual climate of a college or university. The process, the outcomes, and especially the passion of discovery enhance the meaning of the effort and of the institution itself.

Integration, the second of the four forms of scholarship, involves faculty members in overcoming the isolation and fragmentation of the disciplines. The scholarship of integration makes connections within and between the disciplines, altering the contexts in which people view knowledge and offsetting the inclination to split knowledge into ever more esoteric bits and pieces. Often, integrative scholarship educates nonspecialists by giving meaning to isolated facts and putting them in perspective. The scholarship of integration is serious, disciplined work that seeks to interpret, draw together, and bring new insight to bear on original research.

These first two kinds of scholarship—the discovery and integration of knowledge—reflect the investigative and synthesizing traditions of academic life. The third element, the scholarship of application, moves toward engagement as the scholar asks, "How can knowledge be responsibly applied to consequential problems?" Historically, higher learning has been viewed as being useful, "in the nation's service," as Woodrow Wilson put it.[10] Yet this obligation to the larger society should go beyond Wilson's vision of educating future leaders. Colleges and universities also must respond to the issues of the day, following the model set in place more than a century ago by the land-grant colleges as they tried to meet the needs of the nation's farmers. Lessons learned in the application of knowledge can enrich teaching, and new intellectual understandings can arise from the very act of application, whether in medical diagnosis, exploration of an environmental problem, study of a design defect in architecture, or an attempt to apply the latest learning theories in public schools. Theory and practice interact in such ventures and improve each other.

Finally, we come to the scholarship of teaching. Scholarly teaching initiates students into the best values of the academy, enabling them to comprehend better and participate more fully in the larger culture. Teaching also entices future scholars. Robert Oppenheimer, speaking at the two hundredth anniversary of Columbia University, said: "It is proper to the role of the scientist that he not merely find new truth . . . but that he teach, that he try to bring the most honest and intelligible account of new knowledge to all who will try to learn."[11] Reciprocal benefits flow as well to the faculty members who enrich their teaching by building on what they learn in exchanges with students.

Scholarship Reconsidered argued that the academy needs to recognize and reward all four categories of scholarship. We remain persuaded of that proposition. The modern American university has built its distinction on the excellence of the scholarship of discovery. Institutions must remain unfaltering in that commitment. But research alone will not secure the future of higher education, nor of the country at large. Poised on the cusp of a new century, in a world that wrestles with a multitude of difficulties, the university must fulfill a more well-rounded mission. New generations of college-goers need scholarly teachers to help them prepare for a time when global interdependency is much more than a slogan. Knowledge, for all the glory and splendor of the act of pure discovery, remains incomplete without the insights of those who can show how best to integrate and apply it.

Thus, American higher education has to demonstrate the imagination and creativity to support and reward both scholars uniquely gifted in research and those who excel in other uses of knowledge. *Scholarship Reconsidered* suggested that colleges and universities help faculty build on their strengths and sustain their energies by affording them flexible career paths that avoid narrow definitions of scholarship.

A broader definition of scholarship should also enable institutions to define their goals more precisely. Although the full range of scholarship could flourish on a single campus, every college and university should find its own special niche. This may mean that an institution, while recognizing all types of scholarly work, may choose to stress teaching, or application, or integration, or research. Whatever the scholarly emphasis, the approach deserves dignity and respect, insofar as it is performed with distinction. Excellence must be the only yardstick.

A National Conversation

In the years since its publication, *Scholarship Reconsidered* has joined and helped shape a lively debate about the work of faculty. Russell Edgerton, then president of the American Association of Higher Education (AAHE), noted that the report appeared just as the balance between teaching and research was emerging as the subject of a national debate.[12] By identifying the four scholarly functions, *Scholarship Reconsidered* helped refocus the discussion on how faculty roles and institutional missions support, rather than conflict with, each other. The challenge to the academic community was and continues to be the need to expand the definition of legitimate faculty work in ways that put research in proper perspective without doing it harm.

A broader definition of scholarship sets the stage for giving greater legitimacy to activities in which faculty members already engage, even if their institutions do not yet accord their work the rewards it deserves. For example, faculty workloads have been measured in terms of classroom teaching hours for many years. In 1994, however, the American Association of University Professors (AAUP) report *The Work of Faculty* directed "attention to total faculty workload rather than classroom hours." As the authors noted, "The world changes: . . . We now approach the question of balance through definitions of teaching, scholarship, and service that emphasize the great variety of activities so embraced; we urge the integration of *all* the components of academic activity."[13]

Many academicians want the term *scholarship* to have broader implications so that the expertise represented by faculty work other than research is appropriately rewarded. Even the disciplinary and professional societies find this idea intriguing. In an extraordinary venture, Robert Diamond of Syracuse University invited representatives of twenty associations to consider what a larger idea of scholarly activity in their fields might include. Historians; mathematicians; geographers; sociologists; chemists; architects; and faculty in a variety of the visual and performing arts, business, and journalism proposed frameworks to encompass the full range of professional work that scholars might do.[14]

Reports from these fields show how conceptions of scholarship have widened beyond matters limited to the published results of basic research. The mathematicians, for example, proposed to include research in core or applied areas, in mathematical techniques, and in teaching and learning; syntheses of existing scholarship such as surveys, book reviews, and lists of open problems; expositions that communicate mathematics to new audiences and to established audiences with improved clarity; the development of courses, curricula, or instructional materials for grades K–12 as well as college levels; and the development of software that provides tools for research and teaching in mathematics, as well as its application and communication.[15]

Historians, likewise, agreed that scholarship embraced more than published monographs and refereed articles that report on original research. Works of synthesis aimed at nonprofessionals could be scholarly, the historians suggested, and so could such applied activities as public history, including exhibits or tours in museums or other cultural institutions, consulting and providing expert testimony on public policy, participating in film and other media projects, historic preservation and cultural resource management, giving public lectures, and judging history-day competitions. Scholarly work might also include teaching and such associated activities as mentoring and advising, developing curricula and instructional materials, and collaborating with the schools.[16]

Conversations about expanded notions of scholarship continue apace in other venues as well. The themes of some national conferences reflect the larger debate about faculty roles: "The Engaged Campus";[17] "Professors as Citizens: The Academic in Public Life";[18] and, most notably, the series of annual meetings sponsored by the AAHE's Forum on Faculty Roles and Rewards. Oversubscribed for its first meeting, this event grew from 564 participating individuals and teams in 1993 to 1,100 at the fifth meeting in 1997. As R. Eugene Rice, the director of the AAHE Forum, observed: "New issues related to the changing priorities, rewards, and responsibilities of the professoriate are drawn to our attention almost daily. Hundreds of campus projects designed to address these issues are now in place and examples of good practice are readily available."[19]

To obtain a more comprehensive picture of campus activity, The Carnegie Foundation surveyed chief academic officers at all of the country's four-year colleges and universities in the fall of 1994 and found that more than 80 percent of them either had recently reexamined their systems of faculty roles and rewards or planned to do so. More specifically, 21 percent of the provosts said that their institutions had completed reviews during the previous five years, 45 percent said reviews were still under way, and 17 percent expected to initiate reviews soon. Interestingly, the findings were comparable among the various institutional types (Table 1.1).

Our survey found a remarkably similar range of issues under consideration on most campuses. More than half of all institutions wanted to clarify their goals in order to strike a better balance between institutional mission and faculty rewards. At least three-quarters of all institutions hoped to find ways to improve the balance of time and effort faculty spend on various tasks. The most widely embraced goal was to redefine such traditional faculty roles as teaching, research, and service (Table 1.2).

About 80 percent of the provosts reported that the expanded definition of scholarship included the full range of activities in which faculty engage, and a similar number said that the definition of teaching included such activities as curriculum development, advising, and conducting instructional and classroom research. At least half were beginning to distinguish applied scholarship (professional service or outreach) from campus and community citizenship (Table 1.3).

As we argued in *Scholarship Reconsidered,* this is a critically important move. A sharp distinction must be drawn between citizenship activities and projects that relate to scholarship itself. To be sure, there are meritorious social and civic functions to be performed, and faculty should be appropriately recognized for such work. But all too frequently, service means not doing scholarship but doing good. To be considered scholarship, service activities must be tied directly to one's special field of knowledge and relate to, and flow directly out of, this professional activity. Such service is serious, demanding work, requiring the rigor— and the accountability—traditionally associated with research activities.

Table 1.1. In the Past Five Years, Has Your College or
University Reexamined Faculty Roles and Rewards?

	YES, THE REVIEW HAS BEEN COMPLETED	YES, THE REVIEW IS STILL UNDERWAY	NO, BUT WE PLAN TO INITIATE A REVIEW SOON	NO, WE DO NOT PLAN TO INITIATE SUCH A REVIEW SOON
All Institutions	21%	45%	17%	18%
Research	25	48	11	16
Doctorate-Granting	15	55	15	14
Comprehensive	20	47	19	15
Liberal Arts	22	39	17	22

Source: The Carnegie Foundation for the Advancement of Teaching, National Survey on the Reexamination of Faculty Roles and Rewards, 1994.

Table 1.2. Issues Identified as the Focus of Institutional Review
(Percentage Responding "Yes")

	ALL INSTITUTIONS	RESEARCH	DOCTORATE-GRANTING	COMPRE-HENSIVE	LIBERAL ARTS
Clarifying institutional mission	69%	76%	67%	70%	65%
Redefining faculty roles	86	87	96	91	78
Striking a balance between institutional mission and faculty rewards	66	86	80	65	58
Improving the balance of time and effort faculty spend on various tasks	78	76	88	79	76

Source: The Carnegie Foundation for the Advancement of Teaching, National Survey on the Reexamination of Faculty Roles and Rewards, 1994.

Table 1.3. Changes in Institutional Definitions of Faculty Work
(Percentage Responding "Yes")

	ALL INSTITUTIONS	RESEARCH	DOCTORATE-GRANTING	COMPRE-HENSIVE	LIBERAL ARTS
The definition of scholarship is being broadened...	78%	66%	79%	85%	74%
The definition of teaching is being broadened...	80	80	89	80	79
Applied scholarship is being clearly distinguished from citizenship	54	48	55	67	43
The role of faculty as campus citizens is being clarified	64	47	54	69	67

Source: The Carnegie Foundation for the Advancement of Teaching, National Survey on the Reexamination of Faculty Roles and Rewards, 1994.

Although officials at many institutions agree on the importance of enlarging the definition of scholarship, they do not as readily find consensus on matters regarding the reward structure. Campuses have a long way to go before they show that other forms of scholarship receive value equal to that accorded to traditional research. This does not mean efforts to change have been wholly unfruitful. Institutions are clearly enhancing rewards for teaching. More than two-thirds of the campuses in our 1994 survey reported that they provided travel funds for purposes of teaching improvement (79 percent), special awards for teaching excellence (78 percent), sabbaticals for teaching improvement (74 percent), and grants for course development (68 percent) (Table 1.4). Further, some 30 percent of institutions had developed policies to encourage faculty to shift their scholarly focus on occasion, for example concentrating extra time on research for a while and then on teaching. This is a notable beginning in the pursuit of a more balanced definition of scholarship.

Assuring Quality

The move to broaden definitions of scholarship remains uncertain in its potential outcome. Even as the disciplinary associations propose more inclusive definitions of what might count as scholarly work, they insist that assurances of quality must accompany changes. The report of the Joint Policy Board for Mathematics states that "The results of scholarly activities must be public and must be amenable to evaluation."[20]

The Association of American Geographers emphasized that "teaching competence should be verified by rigorous peer review" and that geography programs "develop coherent, systematic plans for evaluating and valuing outreach roles."[21] The American Chemical Society concurred, adding, "The task force recognizes the fact that mechanisms for gauging scholarship outside of research are not generally or firmly in place. We encourage the creative development of new approaches to measure scholarship in chemistry across a broad spectrum of activities."[22]

This concern about quality was already manifest in the efforts of many colleges and universities to give heightened importance to teaching. The Carnegie Foundation's 1994 survey showed widespread experimentation with new evaluation techniques—especially in regard to teaching, where the need for more systematic sources and types of evidence has long been recognized. Across the United States, in fact, over two-thirds of college and university provosts reported that their institutions were developing new methods to evaluate teaching. They were looking in other directions as well. About one-third of the country's colleges and universities reported attempts to fashion new methods for evaluating research, creative work, applied scholarship, and service to the college or profession (Table 1.5).

Table 1.4. New Practices in Place or Being Considered to Reward Good Teaching

	NOW IN PLACE	UNDER CONSIDERATION	NOT UNDER CONSIDERATION
Travel fund for teaching improvement	79%	11%	10%
Special awards for teaching excellence	78	12	10
Sabbaticals for teaching improvement	74	12	14
Grants for course development	68	16	15
Release time for course development	58	18	24
Merit increases for teaching excellence	50	25	25
Using distinguished teachers as mentors	37	39	22
A center for teaching improvement	28	33	37
Distinguished chairs for teaching excellence	23	23	53

Source: The Carnegie Foundation for the Advancement of Teaching, National Survey on the Reexamination of Faculty Roles and Rewards, 1994.

Table 1.5. Areas in Which New Methods of Evaluating Faculty Have Been Developed

(Percentage Responding "Yes")

	ALL INSTITUTIONS	RESEARCH	DOCTORATE-GRANTING	COMPRE-HENSIVE	LIBERAL ARTS
Teaching	69%	77%	66%	66%	70%
Advising	38	28	39	38	41
Research	34	16	33	44	30
Creative work	36	24	31	38	38
Applied scholarship	38	39	47	43	32
Service to the college	42	22	33	46	46
Service to the profession	33	19	30	40	33

Source: The Carnegie Foundation for the Advancement of Teaching, National Survey on the Reexamination of Faculty Roles and Rewards, 1994.

This spate of attention to evaluation is overdue. Many of today's most familiar evaluation procedures were implemented in a hasty response to the very special circumstances of the 1970s. It was a period during which the academy's postwar expansion eased and tenure-track positions became scarce just as larger numbers of women and minorities sought to enter faculty ranks, putting pressure on the appointment process. The "old-boy network" that had long prevailed provided for professors to be appointed and promoted through far more personalized and less formal means than are used now. As recently as the 1960s, even many prestigious liberal arts colleges relied on recommendations from professors at particular graduate schools to identify new faculty candidates. "No outside evaluations were required or expected," wrote Robert McCaughey. "Such procedures and promotion policies provided the maximum assurance that the question 'Does he fit in?' could be answered positively before the college committed itself to a faculty member, and vice versa."[23]

The situation changed markedly at selective liberal arts colleges during the 1970s. Peter Seldin's surveys of practices in faculty evaluation at these institutions documented the shifts. He found that although classroom teaching remained the leading factor in overall evaluation of faculty, research, publication, activity in professional societies, and consultation rose in value. Meanwhile, length of service in rank, competing job offers, and personal attributes counted for less. Indeed, the use of so-called personal attributes, such as the candidate's politics, dress, or friends, declined as factors faster and more precipitously than any others. Seldin cited a dean at a college in Ohio who explained: "Through bitter courtroom experience we've learned that personal attributes won't stand up as the reason to deny a professor tenure. The judge insisted on hard data, but all we could offer were comments about personal attributes. We lost the case."[24]

It was not long before the entire evaluation process became more structured and systematic. By 1983, Seldin could conclude that in the liberal arts colleges "more data sources are being introduced, and the assessment procedures are more open. Although the department chairs and deans are still the predominant sources of information on teaching performance, their grip is loosening. Other data sources—classroom visits, course syllabi and examinations, and self-evaluation— are emerging in importance. Systematic student ratings have become so popular that today they closely trail dean evaluation in importance."[25] Seldin's 1993 survey found that the situation had stabilized to new norms: the changes that took place from 1973 to 1983 had become the status quo in liberal arts colleges.[26]

But shifts occurred in other sorts of institutions, too. Criteria for advancement became more formalized and more complex almost everywhere, earlier at universities and doctoral institutions and later at the comprehensive colleges and smaller institutions. As one overview of faculty evaluation put it, "A trend of the 1970s that has continued into the 1980s has been for colleges and universities to develop faculty evaluation programs that are more systematic and comprehensive than those in the past."[27] There can be no doubt that this change helped open up what was once a fairly closed system, making it easier for women and minority candidates to enter and advance in the professoriate and increasing opportunities for Ph.D.s from newer graduate programs and less prestigious schools.

It is equally clear, however, that the revised system contained flaws. In place of the old unwritten consensus about academic values, a tendency arose to avoid subjective judgments and to try to find ways to make quality seem more objective. The Carnegie Foundation's 1992 International Survey of the Academic Profession found that 45 percent of American professors believed that at their institution "publications used for promotion decisions are just 'counted,' not qualitatively evaluated."[28]

Such practices have invited abuse. Attempts at objectivity led to a system in which activities that were not so easily quantified—teaching, integrative work, and applied work—were avoided as a waste of valuable time. Friends and mentors advised young scholars to fashion their careers with their resumes in mind. We even found a how-to-succeed manual that recommended getting a book out early by looking "for something quick and sure, which may not be really important, but just good enough to get published."[29] Senior scholars, too, sometimes publish simply to impress review committees at funding agencies and at their own colleges or universities. People have grown so eager to associate their names with as many scholarly papers as possible that in some scientific fields papers are signed by one hundred or more authors—everyone, in fact, who contributed in any manner to the research.[30]

When evaluation is obsessed with numbers, it shortchanges teaching and service as well as research. In teaching, this has led to undue emphasis on student course evaluations, which provide a wealth of statistical comparisons and measures. And it has contributed to the undervaluation of professional service because virtually no institution has yet figured out how to quantify such work. It is not surprising that public service and consultation ranked extremely low as factors used in evaluating the overall quality of faculty in liberal arts colleges[31] or that over 70 percent of American professors have said that "better ways to evaluate teaching performance" are needed at their institutions.[32]

Certainly, the move to broaden scholarship has called new attention to the imperative for better assessment—evidence and standards that allow colleagues to make reliable judgments about quality without overreliance on quantification. It is widely recognized that new means of evaluation are essential to foster first-rate research and creative work and to encourage and reward scholarly teaching and professional service. A task force on the reward system at the University of California, San Diego, for example, concluded that "to do proper justice to teaching and service contributions within the reward system, it is necessary to develop evaluation criteria and documentation methods to supplement those now in use."[33] Ball State University pointed out that a pluralistic approach to faculty scholarship requires "each faculty member . . . to communicate clearly his or her goals and accomplishments to those judging for tenure, promotion, and merit salary increases."[34]

Our own experience attests both to the seriousness of the problem and to the necessity for change. *Scholarship Reconsidered* was well received on many campuses that were struggling to rethink faculty roles and rewards. The report was recommended reading for faculty and administrators involved in these conversations. But as useful as the book may have been for stimulating discussion about the nature of academic work, the fact remains that it had little to say about the practical issues facing campus committees charged with bringing about change. The ink was barely dry when we started to get calls and letters that said, in effect, "It's one thing to give scholarship a larger meaning, but the real issue revolves around how to assess other forms of scholarship."

During the last half century, the United States built what is unquestionably the most remarkable network of institutions of higher learning in the world. Now, though, this marvelous array of colleges and universities must adjust to new realities in an era of scarcity and rising expectations. The golden age of expansion for colleges and universities lingers as a memory. Richard Atkinson and Donald Tuzin have written that the time has come "to restore the structural balances through which the university attunes itself to a changing world."[35]

The continued vitality of the nation's colleges and universities in the approaching century depends on their ability to show more care for a wider range of missions. As a correlate, they must embrace a broader vision of scholarship to better align faculty roles with institutional goals. Otherwise, higher education ends up paying only lip service to faculty activities that it is not prepared to reward.

Realization of this vision demands new ways of evaluating scholarly work, so as to ensure its quality and fully legitimate its different forms. One distinguished professor at a prestigious liberal arts college told us, "As a faculty member who has been rigid about the role of 'traditional research,' I find my position much softened as long as the issue of scholarly rigor is being upheld." This is, of course, our point.

CHAPTER TWO

Standards of Scholarly Work

To give the four kinds of scholarly activities the weight that each deserves, they all must be held to the same standards of scholarly performance. The paradox is this: in order to recognize discovery, integration, application, and teaching as legitimate forms of scholarship, the academy must evaluate them by a set of standards that capture and acknowledge what they share as scholarly acts.

Faculty handbooks seldom highlight the qualities and characteristics common to the different kinds of scholarship. Rather, current wisdom assumes that research, teaching, and applied scholarship—the kinds of faculty activities recognized for purposes of evaluation on most campuses—each has its own special yardstick.

In judging research, each discipline uses its own criteria, while estimates of teaching abilities tend to ignore strategies specific to subject matter. Service is in a league of its own. The activities that count as professional and/or public service may be identified, but aside from the general expectation of "high quality" in such work, handbooks offer scant guidance as to what quality might mean. Indeed, the University of California is unusual in its thoughtful requirements for practitioners in its professional schools. It singles out "leadership in the field" and "demonstrated progressiveness in the development or utilization of new approaches and techniques for the solution of professional problems."[1]

Most college and university guidebooks implicitly suggest that different *types* of standards apply to different kinds of faculty work, leaving the impression that standards for research and creative work come from the various disciplines; standards for teaching are institutionally defined; and standards for professional service vary so greatly by project and profession that hardly any guidance can be offered. This fragmented paradigm reflects the differential respect accorded research, teaching, and applied scholarship at most institutions. It also, we believe, helps to perpetuate the hierarchy that places greatest importance on research. As Lee Shulman observed, "Like it or not, the forms of scholarship that are seen as intellectual work in the disciplines are going to be valued more than forms of scholarship (such as teaching) that are seen as non-disciplinary."[2] One can understand how teaching and applied work often suffer devaluation in this taxonomy of unequals.

In recent years, though, academics have opened discussion about standards for teaching and applied scholarship at both the national and campus levels. The disciplinary associations have begun to address this issue. The American Mathematical Society, for example, has pioneered an ambitious program to improve the teaching of calculus and to define the qualities of good undergraduate teaching in mathematics. Scholars doing applied work in most of the humanities and social sciences are organizing sessions at disciplinary conferences and airing substantive methodological and ethical concerns in newsletters and journals. Even integrative scholarship claims the attention of growing numbers of disciplinary peers; for instance, the *Journal of American History* now regularly reviews museum exhibitions. "Museum exhibits and their related elements are a distinct medium for identifying, organizing, comparing, analyzing, and communicating historical information and interpretation," the editor of the reviews wrote.[3]

The emerging climate at colleges and universities supports the idea that different types of scholarly work merit formal consideration. In experiments across the country, faculty are assembling a wide variety of evidence to demonstrate their achievements in the four areas of scholarship. Many institutions are also trying to improve how peers are brought into the review of teaching. Shulman captures the mood precisely when he speaks of making teaching "community property,"[4] while the aptly titled theme of the 1995 AAHE Conference on Faculty Roles and Rewards was "From 'My Work' to 'Our Work.'"[5]

Reform, however, seldom moves evenly on all fronts, and innovative attempts to broaden definitions of scholarship are likely to remain pilot efforts if institutions do not also change the standards by which they evaluate scholarship for purposes of faculty retention, promotion, and tenure. As Richard Chait noted, recognizing different forms of scholarship involves "less certainty about the qualities and characteristics of scholarship—about what should count."[6] Clearly, evaluation that uses different standards for research, teaching, and professional service has outlived its day. Academia needs a single standard, but it cannot implement that standard simply by applying to other forms of scholarship the traditional criteria that have usually been used for judging research.

What are the common features that enable scholars involved in different fields of study and different types of scholarly work to feel they are engaged in a common task? Wayne Booth observed that the academic world has an evaluative language beyond the disciplinary or professional rhetoric of the cutting edge. Booth said that faculty already can use this common evaluative language to ask if a colleague's "style of presentation . . . accords with standards we recognize," to examine the general quality of someone's reasoning, and to see whether talking with a colleague adds to one's own intellectual life.[7]

Could there lie in this public square some clues that might help us find a vocabulary to define the common dimensions of scholarship? Are there already some general standards available for judging scholarly performance?

In an attempt to answer these essential questions, we accumulated a voluminous file of documents, including guidelines on hiring, tenure, and promotion practices from dozens of colleges and universities. We also got responses from fifty-one granting agencies and from editors and directors of thirty-one scholarly journals and fifty-eight university presses whom we asked about the standards they use to decide the scholarly merit of proposals and manuscripts. In addition, we collected many of the forms that institutions provide to students and occasionally to faculty peers to evaluate college teaching.

Ostensibly, these lists of standards and criteria vary considerably. Some are long, some short. Some are systematic, some jumbled. Many include items tailored to specific needs. The National Science Foundation, for instance, is interested in the effect a proposed project might have on the infrastructure of science and engineering.[8] Before publishing an article, the *Journal of Organic Chemistry* wants to know if the compounds reported are "adequately characterized with regard to identity and purity";[9] the University of California Press, as many other university publishers, asks hopefully: is a manuscript "likely to be required reading in specific undergraduate or graduate courses?"[10]

The most remarkable feature of these various guidelines, though, is not how much they contain that is unique but the degree to which they share elements. Our survey of standards indicates that the key to these commonalities lies in the *process* of scholarship itself. If this process can be defined with some clarity, it will provide terms by which scholars can discuss almost any project without denying either its uniqueness or its connections to other projects, whatever the discipline or type of scholarship. Indeed, we found it possible to identify in these lists and guidelines a set of six shared themes. All works of scholarship, be they discovery, integration, application, or teaching, involve a common sequence of unfolding stages. We have found that when people praise a work of scholarship, they usually mean that the project in question shows that it has been guided by these qualitative standards:

1. Clear goals

2. Adequate preparation

3. Appropriate methods

4. Significant results

5. Effective presentation

6. Reflective critique

It is important, we believe, to give these familiar standards—already in common use—explicit articulation. Everyone will recognize them one by one, but taken together, they provide a powerful conceptual framework to guide evaluation. Their very obviousness suggests their applicability to a broad range of intellectual projects.

Clear Goals

A scholar must be clear about the aims of his or her work. The first issue that many reviewers are asked to address in their evaluations of manuscripts and grant or fellowship proposals concerns the scholar's goals. The *American Journal of Sociology* asks, "Is an important issue being addressed?"[11] The Johns Hopkins University Press, in its review of a scholarly manuscript, inquires, "What is the author's goal?"[12] The journal *Environmental Science and Technology* wants to know, "Is the basic question to be addressed clearly stated?"[13]

We also found a strong emphasis on goals when it comes to assessing teaching. One evaluation instrument asks, "Did the professor clearly state the objectives of the course?" Another wants to know, "Did the proposed objectives agree with those actually taught?" At the University of Kentucky, professors being reviewed for promotion and tenure are asked to submit a brief, reflective statement that sets forth their philosophy and objectives as teachers.[14] The clarity of goals was considered for works of applied scholarship as well. The National Institute of Justice, which funds projects for the U.S. Department of Justice, wants to know, "Does the proposal address a critical issue or aspect of the problem area?"[15]

These, then, are questions that ought to be asked about all types of scholarly work:

- Does the scholar state the basic purposes of his or her work clearly?

- Does the scholar define objectives that are realistic and achievable?

- Does the scholar identify important questions in the field?

Goals precede all other considerations because to plan, carry out, and present any scholarly project, a scholar must know what questions to ask. A master scholar is a master question-raiser—a designation that fits, almost by definition, anyone who can be called a pathbreaker in scholarly and creative work. The most basic lessons taught to students in their graduate training involve learning how to see and state an intellectual problem. The Council of Graduate Schools noted in describing the nature and purpose of doctoral programs: "A well-prepared doctoral student will have developed the ability . . . to apply appropriate principles and procedures to the recognition, evaluation, interpretation, and understanding of issues and problems at the frontiers of knowledge."[16]

Scholarly work usually has multiple goals, making it crucial that the scholar define each goal clearly within *all* relevant contexts, disciplinary or interdisciplinary, public or professional, and educational as well. For example, a teacher may select an intellectually significant problem for a new course but teach poorly because of ill-defined pedagogical goals. "Bad teaching most often results from a pursuit of the wrong ends, either because the teacher is unclear about his or her purposes or because plausible but harmful purposes get in the way of good ones," Booth observed.[17] Only by stating objectives clearly can the stage be set for conversations about appropriateness of goals.

Having clear goals also means understanding a project's scope. Good guiding questions help the scholar define a project, give it structure, recognize relevant material, identify exceptions, and see new possibilities. Of course, the goals of a project may shift over time. Much of the excitement of scholarly work comes when a particular line of inquiry leads to new questions and these lead to new ones again.

A scholar's goals must also be realistic, taking account of the limitations and the possibilities of the situation. Hopelessly grandiose goals may fade into irrelevancy. Goals should be practical and defensible. Even clear objectives hold little value if they cannot be reasonably met.

Adequate Preparation

The documents we examined repeatedly identified adequate preparation as one of the most basic aspects of scholarly work. The University of Alabama Press, for example, asks this question of reviewers: "Does the scholarship appear current?"[18] In other words, has the scholar's preparation for the investigation adequately considered the state of the field? The University Press of New England asks, "Is the author in command of both primary sources and the standard secondary literature of the field?"[19] Regarding teaching, one evaluation instrument we looked at asks, "Did the instructor display a clear understanding of the course topics?" and "Was the instructor well prepared for each class?" Agencies that support applied projects agree. The Mott Foundation, for example, wants to know: "Does the applicant have the leadership and staff competence to carry out the project, or the ability to secure those essential resources?"[20]

Any evaluation should consider the following questions when assessing a scholar's achievements:

- Does the scholar show an understanding of existing scholarship in the field?
- Does the scholar bring the necessary skills to his or her work?
- Does the scholar bring together the resources necessary to move the project forward?

The pursuit of scholarly work depends, fundamentally, on the depth and breadth of the scholar's understanding of subject matter. Every scholar bears a responsibility to keep up with the literature in the field in which he or she works. Scholarship is, in essence, a conversation in which one participates and contributes by knowing what is being discussed and what others have said on the subject. Therefore, a project that does not speak to current issues of theory, fact, interpretation, or method is unlikely to contribute to its field, regardless of other virtues.

Artistry necessarily accompanies knowledge in the projects a scholar undertakes. All scholarly work involves practical skills and rules of thumb that one usually learns by doing and by observing the work of others. This is what Shulman called "the wisdom of practice" in teaching, what Donald Schön described as "reflection-in-action" in applied work, and what C. Wright Mills called "the practice of a craft" in research.[21] Such know-how is crucial even in the heartland of basic science, the laboratory itself, where, as Jacob Bronowski observes, "the skill of head and hand go together."[22] Mastery of necessary skills should be taken into account in evaluating a scholarly project.

Professional preparation also requires one to ascertain the availability of the right resources for the project at hand. A scholar, in weighing the human resources, should know who is doing similar work, who is supporting such work, and who is interested in the findings. A particular project might require, for example, such background work as learning a new language or exploring new software. Resources, of course, can determine the success or failure of a project, and questions about resources are pertinent in evaluating adequacy of preparation. Was the scholar imaginative and thorough in finding source material? Were the resources adequate for the project? Did the scholar use the resources as well as possible?

Appropriate Methods

As a third standard, scholars also must use procedures appropriate to the project, choosing methods wisely, applying them effectively, and modifying them judiciously as a project evolves. Virtually all evaluating agencies inquire into the merit of a scholar's methods. The University of Iowa Press, in judging a scholarly manuscript, asks, "Is the scholarship adequate in terms of methodology?"[23] The journal *Physical Review Letters* expresses it this way: "Is the work scientifically sound?"[24] The journal *Child Development* urges reviewers to consider "the formal design of the research," that is, its methodology.[25] Kansas State University judges the quality of projects in terms of the "development and application of effective ways to identify problems and assess needs."[26]

Methods and procedures make a great difference in teaching. This is true from the logic of the syllabus to pedagogical procedures and student assessment. One teacher evaluation instrument asks, "Were the methods of evaluating student work fair and effective?" Another wants to know, "Was the amount of material the instructor attempted to cover appropriate?" Students at Clemson University are asked whether the course was "presented in a logical sequence."[27] The State University of New York College at Old Westbury looks at the professor's "responsiveness to the distinctive and varied needs of our students" and "successful experimentation with varied approaches to teaching."[28]

We suggest, then, that evaluators ask these questions about a scholar's work:

- Does the scholar use methods appropriate to the goals?
- Does the scholar apply effectively the methods selected?
- Does the scholar modify procedures in response to changing circumstances?

At the most basic level, appropriate methodology gives a project integrity and engenders confidence in its findings, products, or results. To gain standing among scholars, a project must use methods recognized in the academic community. Edward Shils said: "The obligations of the academic profession are inherent in the custodianship of the pursuit, acquisition, assessment, and transmission of knowledge through systematic study, in accordance with methodical procedures including observational techniques, rules of evidence, and principles of logical reasoning."[29] Shils's observation is most obvious in scientific research, where reason and experiment have often defined what science is and what it is not. All fields of scholarly inquiry are both theoretical and methodical, although the method may not be the kind of controlled observation that the phrase *scientific method* usually conveys.

The choice of method is critical because upon it depends not only the project's chances for success at discovery, integration, application, or teaching but also the likelihood that colleagues will understand and accept the project. Scholars who favor quantitative studies, for example, may be reluctant to accept findings based on qualitative approaches, whatever the intrinsic merit of the work. Yet all scholars would probably concede the value of approaches other than their own, however incompatible the methodological styles. They might argue for the primacy of one approach or another, but most important is that the method selected be carefully justified and appropriate to the project's goals.

Scholars have an obligation to carry out their projects competently. To expect a project to unfold according to the method outlined, however, is not to ask a scholar to follow blindly a detailed, preconceived plan. Scholarship does not and should not proceed like that. Flexibility is essential to allow the scholar to respond to change, to pick up a clue and follow it as a project proceeds, and even to redesign the project itself. C. Wright Mills advised the young scholar to "be a good craftsman: Avoid any rigid set of procedures . . . let theory and method again become part of the practice of a craft."[30] This admonition holds for the mature scholar as well.

Significant Results

Any act of scholarship must also be judged by the significance of its results. A project should contribute to knowledge or to artistic expression, stimulate learning, or, where appropriate, help solve problems outside the academy. Publishers and journal editors are invariably direct about this standard when they consider manuscripts reporting findings from research. The University of Hawaii Press asks, "What has the author accomplished?"[31] The University of Arizona Press wants to know if the manuscript "makes a significant contribution to the literature."[32] And the *Journal of Physical Chemistry* asks if the manuscript has "extremely important results."[33] The scholarship of application also is judged by outcomes. At the University of Illinois, peers are asked to comment on the extent to which a colleague's service activity has made a substantial contribution that is "recognized by other scholars, public policy makers, or practitioners."[34]

Teaching, too, must in the end be judged not merely by process but by results, however eloquent a teacher's performance. The evaluation forms we studied ask students questions that clearly seek to measure the significance of what they learned: "Was your interest in the subject stimulated by this course?" "Did you improve your competence due to this course?" "Did you learn something you consider valuable?"

The following questions, we believe, help colleagues chart the significance of a scholar's work:

- Does the scholar achieve the goals?

- Does the scholar's work add consequentially to the field?

- Does the scholar's work open additional areas for further exploration?

To ask that the outcome of a scholarly project have significance is to ask, first, that it meet its own goals. Its results, in other words, should have meaning within the parameters that the scholar has set for the project. A course in which students conduct their own research under faculty supervision should show evidence that students gained insights into methods of investigation. A consultation should actually help clients while contributing to the scholar's understanding of the general issues involved. Experiments that aim to unearth new findings should in fact do so—even, of course, when the findings simply eliminate a hypothesis by concluding that "no significant difference was found." A book designed to introduce an arcane topic to a nonacademic audience should reach that group of readers with the requisite integrity, imagination, and style.

A fundamental indication of a project's significance is its contribution to the field. Chemist-philosopher Michael Polanyi once suggested that scientists typically judged scientific research by its plausibility, originality, and scientific value—"a composite," explained science writer Richard Rhodes, "consisting of equal parts accuracy, importance to the entire system of whatever branch of science the idea belonged to, and intrinsic interest."[35] Many scholars use some variant of this scheme in judging a work's contribution. Of course, the language of praise varies among the disciplines. Anthropologist Clifford Geertz observed that mathematicians speak of the differences between "'deep,' 'elegant,' 'beautiful,' 'powerful,' and 'subtle' proofs"; physicists talk of "such peculiar words of praise and blame as 'tact' or 'skimming'"; and literary critics invoke "the relative presence of a mysterious property, to outsiders anyway, called 'realization.'"[36] Significance in these instances takes on a meaning and appreciation specific to a field, attesting to the need to acknowledge the specialized nature that significance may sometimes assume.

Clearly, teaching, integration, and application can contribute to their own scholarly realms. For example, a new way of teaching undergraduate calculus might serve as a model for colleagues at the same institution or beyond. A diagnostic method developed by a clinician-scholar might influence practitioners. The results of a scholar's integrative efforts might help shape public debate and broaden understanding of the issues at hand. Because the four types of scholarship dynamically interact, their contributions to each other can be traced as well. New developments in research, for instance, can contribute to ideas about teaching or application, while ideas generated in teaching, integration, or application can suggest new lines of research.

Finally, when thinking about significance, one can note works of scholarship that, through some happy combination of freshness and timing, open whole new areas for further expansion. Certainly, originality increases the potential for breaking new ground. As Oliver Sacks, a neurologist, noted, "Creativity in this sense involves the power to originate, to break away from the existing ways of looking at things. . . ."[37] Such a project may have an early and obvious impact when the timing is right, attracting an important audience, compelling assent, or stirring debate. Breakthroughs like these are best known in the scholarship of discovery and the scholarship of application, but why should they not also occur when teaching and integrative scholarship become community property?

Effective Presentation

The contribution made by any form of scholarship relies on its presentation. Scholarship, however brilliant, lacks fulfillment without someone on the receiving end. The discovery should be made known to more than the discoverer; teaching is not teaching without students; integration makes scant contribution unless it is communicated so that people may benefit from it; and application becomes application by addressing others' needs.

The criteria used by scholarly presses and professional journals invariably refer to effective communication. Cambridge University Press simply asks, "Is the manuscript well written?"[38] The University Press of Kansas wants to know, "Is the writing style effective?"[39] The *Journal of the American Mathematical Society* says, "Papers must be written clearly," and then adds this fascinating comment: "At least the referee should be able to understand them without undue difficulty."[40] It also says that the paper must be of interest to an appropriate number of readers—not just to the authors, students, and a few colleagues—suggesting that the intended audience of scholarship should be reasonably broad. In this spirit, Kent State University Press asks, "Would there be interest in this book beyond its specialist field?"[41]

The scholarship of application, too, adheres to this standard. The National Academy Press asks, "Are sensitive policy issues treated with proper care?"[42] The Mott Foundation prefers to fund applied projects that "contain an appropriate plan for . . . reporting and dissemination."[43] And the University of Georgia says in its Guidelines for Faculty Appointment, Promotion, and Tenure that the effectiveness of public service should be judged, at least in part, on "the quality and impact of the written documents produced."[44]

The importance of presentation is readily apparent when it comes to teaching. The evaluation forms for teaching that we studied are full of such questions as "Did the instructor speak with good expression?" "Did the teacher explain course material clearly?" "Did the instructor introduce stimulating ideas?" The scholarship of teaching should lead to communication with colleagues, as well as with students. In this spirit, we agree with those colleges and universities that take as an indicator of excellence in teaching the sharing of innovative instructional materials and concepts through formal publications, conferences, and seminars, as well as through more informal means.

In reviewing a scholar's work, these questions should be asked about presentation:

- Does the scholar use a suitable style and effective organization to present his or her work?

- Does the scholar use appropriate forums for communicating work to its intended audiences?

- Does the scholar present his or her message with clarity and integrity?

Good presentation involves a sense of audience and careful attention to the best ways of reaching each of its members. The presentation of scholarship is a public act, and although some work is highly esoteric, it must ultimately be known and understood by at least the members of that special audience. Quite simply, scholars must communicate well. Teaching, for instance, should use images, metaphors, analogies, and examples that connect the subject matter to who the students are and how students learn. A teacher should also take advantage of special opportunities, what educator Parker Palmer calls "critical moments." The first day of class, the first grades awarded, confusion over a key concept, or a disagreement, all offer occasions "when a learning opportunity will either open up or shut down for your students—depending, in part, on how you respond."[45]

The scholarship of application typically calls for communication with practitioners or even public audiences who bring little specialized knowledge to the table. Effective presentation to such groups may require the scholar to learn the different communicative styles of government officials, corporate officers, for-profit laboratory researchers, documentary filmmakers, or primary and secondary school teachers and principals. This may involve media relations and learning how to present one's views in radio and television interviews or through op-ed columns and magazines of general circulation. Effective presentation under these circumstances may require the scholar to do more listening than speaking, recognizing that what the audience says is part of communication. Physicist Freeman Dyson recalls the lengthy process by which a local community was persuaded to permit its resident university to build a laboratory for recombinant DNA research. A series of hearings enabled questioners and critics to have their say and, perhaps, to influence the final outcome. As Dyson noted: "The first lesson that we learned was the importance of listening. The only effective way to dissipate distrust is for the people who are distrusted to sit down and listen to what their critics have to say."[46]

Teaching and applied scholarship can remain incomplete acts unless presentation at some point reaches beyond students, clients, or the public in order to connect with colleagues. Shulman argues that work that is valued is work that is presented to colleagues.[47] The failure to make this kind of wider connection weakens the sense of community. This happens in scholarly life when such essential functions as professional service or teaching do not get discussed openly or often enough. It also occurs when the standards of scholarly communication are poor.

The printed page remains the most common forum by which scholarly work reaches beyond the library, laboratory, seminar room, or conference hall. Unfortunately, though, standards of writing in many academic circles are low. Jargon and obtuse prose deprive scholars of the benefit of the interplay that could result from more effective presentation. If scholars present their work in language as clear and simple as the subject allows, scholarly communication would be improved not only among colleagues but with the public as well. Patricia Nelson Limerick said:

> The redemption of the university, especially in terms of the public's appraisal of the value of research and publication, requires all the writers who have something they want to publish to ask themselves the question: Does this have to be a closed communication, shutting out all but specialists willing to fight their way through thickets of jargon? Or can this be an open communication, engaging specialists with new information and new thinking, but also offering an invitation to nonspecialists to learn from this study, to grasp its importance and, by extension, to find concrete reasons to see value in the work of the university?[46]

Scholars, as a result of technological advances, can increasingly present their work in nontraditional forms. Scholarly communication now flows through electronic networks, where standards for what to say and how to say it are closer to those for oral communication. Scholarly work is also carried by film and television, in the popular press, and even in Hollywood, where academic specialists consult on the lives and times of historical figures, the habits of dinosaurs, and the lives of scholars themselves—witness the portrayal of Robert Oppenheimer in *Fat Man and Little Boy* and the depiction of C. S. Lewis in *Shadowlands*. Museums and galleries display scholarly and creative work; dramatists and musicians from the academy perform in theaters and concert halls.

Popularization, done well, brings together the right materials creatively and helps the audience, whether they be students, clients, the public, or colleagues, appreciate the complexities and importance of the problems addressed in the particular field. In all scholarly work—including that which passes into the popular domain—evidence, analysis, interpretation, and argument should be handled carefully and honestly.

Reflective Critique

Our final standard involves the scholar thinking about his or her work, seeking the opinions of others, and learning from this process so that scholarship itself can be improved. We found little evidence that this standard figures prominently in the evaluation of scholarship as matters now stand, although it is recognized when funding agencies insist on plans for project evaluation, and by colleges or universities that encourage professional development. Nonetheless, the following questions are important to ask:

- Does the scholar critically evaluate his or her own work?

- Does the scholar bring an appropriate breadth of evidence to his or her critique?

- Does the scholar use evaluation to improve the quality of future work?

Throughout history, the ideal of scholarship has been shadowed by the hazard of pedantry. For many, it is wisdom that makes the difference. For example, Abraham Ibn Ezra, the twelfth-century Jewish polymath, warned that "a scholar of the traditional text, who learns nothing else, is like a camel carrying a load of silk: silk and camel are of no use to each other."[49] In the nineteenth century, Ralph Waldo Emerson saw "thinking" as the scholar's true calling,[50] and in our own century C. Wright Mills referred to the "imagination" of the scholar.[51]

Reflection gives the lie to the common but unflattering characterization of scholars as narrow specialists, unable or unwilling to emerge from the depths of their subspecialties for a breath of fresh air. Biologist Barbara McClintock, for example, always urged harried young scientists, rushing on to the next experiment, to "take the time and look."[52] With proper reflection, a scholar can examine his or her project from multiple perspectives—moving more easily beyond the narrow confines within which work in the academy is sometimes observed. The aim is to summon the muses, give free play to intuition—and then take that intuition and clothe it in thought that leads to the next step in one's scholarly career.

Through reflection comes creativity. This ability to invent, devise, envisage, and improvise, is the key to success in all types of scholarly work. Indeed, in his recent study *Making the Case for Professional Service,* Ernest Lynton sees creativity as the essential, and perhaps even defining, characteristic of scholarship. According to Lynton, scholarship is the "antithesis of rote and routine. . . . Scholarly work is not carrying out a recurring task according to a prescribed protocol, applying standard methodologies. What unifies the activities of a scholar, whether engaged in teaching, research, or professional service, is an approach to each task as a novel situation, a voyage of exploration into the partially unknown."[53]

The work of Donald Schön, in particular, draws attention to the extent to which effective professional practice depends not only on how tasks are approached and problems defined but also on how work proceeds. Effective professionals think about what they are doing while they are carrying out their work. And what is true of professional work generally applies to scholarship as well. Its practice requires reflection as the project unfolds so as to adapt to changing circumstances and come to a successful solution. As Schön writes in his influential book *The Reflective Practitioner,* the professional is "open to the situation's back-talk."[54] Scholars, too, recognize and respond to whatever is unique and unexpected in carrying out their work.

Insightful reflection involves self-awareness that continues after the completion of a project. An appropriate plan of inquiry should allow for evaluation, guiding the scholar's thinking about what went right and what went wrong, what opportunities were taken, and which ones were missed. As part of the evaluation, a scholar should solicit opinions and show the ability to respond positively to criticism. Finally, a scholar might follow through with activities enabling the development of new skills or knowledge: attending a program at the institution's center for the improvement of teaching, participating in a workshop on a new research technique, taking time to familiarize oneself with a new body of literature or to design a new course.

In the end, reflective critique both promises and promotes intellectual engagement. It leads to better scholarship. Careful evaluation and constructive criticism enrich scholarly work by enabling old projects to inform new ones. It is precisely the reflection encouraged by these activities that connects separate projects and makes them integral parts of some larger intellectual quest. As the scholar turns to the next research task, the next article, the next course or consultation, older projects feed ideas to the new ones, while the new ones return the favor and enrich the range of implications of those that came before.

We conclude, then, that there is a common language in which to discuss the standards for scholarly work of all kinds, a language that enables us to see clearly what discovery, integration, application, and teaching share as scholarly activities. We acknowledge that these six standards—clear goals, adequate preparation, appropriate methods, significant results, effective presentation, and reflective critique (see Exhibit 2.1)—define phases of an intellectual process that are in reality not so neatly categorized. Still, we find value in analyzing the qualities that scholars admire in finished work, while conceding the playful, anarchic, and unpredictable aspects of the life of the mind. Confidence in the assessment of scholarship depends on using standards that are appropriate to the full range of scholarly work.

Exhibit 2.1. Summary of Standards

Clear Goals

Does the scholar state the basic purposes of his or her work clearly? Does the scholar define objectives that are realistic and achievable? Does the scholar identify important questions in the field?

Adequate Preparation

Does the scholar show an understanding of existing scholarship in the field? Does the scholar bring the necessary skills to his or her work? Does the scholar bring together the resources necessary to move the project forward?

Appropriate Methods

Does the scholar use methods appropriate to the goals? Does the scholar apply effectively the methods selected? Does the scholar modify procedures in response to changing circumstances?

Significant Results

Does the scholar achieve the goals? Does the scholar's work add consequentially to the field? Does the scholar's work open additional areas for further exploration?

Effective Presentation

Does the scholar use a suitable style and effective organization to present his or her work? Does the scholar use appropriate forums for communicating work to its intended audiences? Does the scholar present his or her message with clarity and integrity?

Reflective Critique

Does the scholar critically evaluate his or her own work? Does the scholar bring an appropriate breadth of evidence to his or her critique? Does the scholar use evaluation to improve the quality of future work?

CHAPTER THREE

Documenting Scholarship

THE QUALITY of a faculty member's performance in any of the four areas of scholarship can best be assessed on the basis of evidence that speaks directly to the standards for judging the work. Such documentation requires rich and varied materials that the scholar and others assemble over time to make the case on the scholar's behalf.

It takes imagination and discipline to demonstrate that a project had clear goals and was adequately prepared, that it was conducted with appropriate methods and led to significant results, and that it was presented effectively and reflectively critiqued. Thus, documentation to an agreed-upon set of standards can aid the scholar's reflection, informing the revision of old projects, the conduct of current ones, and plans for new work.

Thoughtful educators have long believed that documentation, done well, promotes better scholarship by engaging scholars more actively in making the case for their achievements. Russell Edgerton, Pat Hutchings, and Kathleen Quinlan suggest that documenting teaching more thoughtfully at the college and university level can "prompt more reflective practice and improvement" and "foster a culture of teaching and a new discourse about it."[1] Surely, as these authors observe, this notion also holds true for the other types of scholarly work.

The biggest challenge that a broadened view of scholarship poses for documentation concerns the types and sources of materials that provide evidence of quality. Simply put, some scholarly activities are more readily documented than others. The scholarship of discovery, with its established system of peer review, especially falls into this category. Grants that were approved by panels of specialists, articles published in refereed journals, and books that were subject to peer review speak to the fact that the scholar's research has *already* been deemed worthy by colleagues. Books and articles intended for a scholarly audience can easily be submitted to review committees, as can evidence of the extent of their impact through such means as book reviews, citation counts, and solicited evaluations from specialists attesting to the cumulative weight of a scholar's contribution.

Many scholarly activities are not so easily reviewed. The countless hours of preparation and follow-through required for teaching find their chief outlet with students in the classroom, laboratory, or office, and not in print. Applied scholarship often results in spoken advice to clients rather than a publication. Although integrative scholarship sometimes appears in books or journals addressed to colleagues, it may also come out in public lectures, magazine articles, radio and television interviews, or museum exhibits—not the stuff around which departmental evaluations usually revolve. Michael Bérubé of the University of Illinois at Urbana-Champaign put it this way: ". . . if I am going to be a responsible professional and professor, I make my work available to the clients of my university and of my discipline; to some extent—as a teacher, as a citizen, as a professional—I take the shape of my container."[2] That container is not always the peer-reviewed article or book.

Institutions and departments that are serious about expanding the scope of scholarship must acknowledge that scholarly work does not always adorn itself in the traditional cap and gown. The new field of public history provides a case in point. A number of history departments have initiated public history programs and have even agreed to new criteria for tenure and promotion for public historians. However, as Kendrick A. Clements pointed out, "problems begin when it comes time to apply the new criteria in specific cases. Confronted with strange-looking materials like environmental impact statements, museum displays, or historic structure reports, academics often respond suspiciously."[3]

Documentation must be opened to a more eclectic array of materials in order to treat newer forms of scholarship fairly. This would mean including more genres of published and unpublished work.[4] Indeed, to capture the variety of media that scholars use to reach particular audiences, documentation need not even be limited to the written word. One should also think more creatively about evidence showing the impact of scholarly work. Samples of students' work or invitations to speak about one's projects might well fit this bill. Finally, it is important to recognize that appropriate and credible reviewers may be found not only among fellow specialists and current students but also among former students, clients, nonacademic authorities, and practitioners in the field.

Broadening the scope of documentation should make it easier to describe a variety of academic projects, while also enhancing the validity and reliability of the evidence. As a particularly thoughtful guide to faculty evaluation prepared at Kansas State University puts it, "Single data sources are best conceptualized as yielding pieces of circumstantial evidence, no one of which is persuasive by itself. However, when multiple data sources are consistent in what they indicate, they can be taken more seriously. This is especially true if the sources of evidence are dissimilar in nature."[5]

Certainly, there has long been agreement that documentation of teaching should be more imaginative, drawing upon many types and sources of evidence, not just a collection of syllabi for example, or data from student rating forms. The term *portfolio* has most often been used to evoke the idea of a file that presents rich and varied materials about a professor's teaching.[6] Sometimes, too, the portfolio idea is extended to documentation of applied scholarship and other types of scholarly work.[7]

The portfolio literature has deepened understanding about how the scholarship of teaching especially might be captured in material form. Edgerton, Hutchings, and Quinlan suggest more than *four dozen* items to consider for submission as part of a teaching portfolio. The authors propose, for example, that a scholar might offer students' test scores, laboratory workbooks, and essays as products of teaching, as well as lists of course materials that one has prepared and a record of research that one has conducted on one's own teaching.[8] Videotapes, too, can prove valuable.

The Carnegie Foundation's 1994 National Survey on the Reexamination of Faculty Roles and Rewards shows that many colleges and universities are seeking a wider range of evidence about teaching, research, and applied scholarship. This can be seen in the relatively high percentages of institutions making use of or considering peer reviews of syllabi, examinations, and other teaching materials (91 percent; Table 3.1), self-evaluations or personal statements about research (86 percent; Table 3.2), and client or user evaluation of applied projects (58 percent; Table 3.3).

The variety of materials that campuses and portfolio advocates are exploring suggests that there are many creative ways to document scholarly performance, but we are concerned about the potential for a lack of selectivity and coherence. The expansion of possibilities for documentation can result in scholars having to devote more and more time to assembling dossiers. Furthermore, this can place greater demands on the time of peers who provide reviews of the candidate's portfolio and on colleagues sitting on evaluation committees, who must sort through the materials in order to reach their decisions. There is also a tendency, according to Edgerton, to turn "to portfolios as the latest management fad without careful thought as to what the contents of portfolios might be."[9]

As its main goal, documentation should provide evidence that enables the scholar and his or her colleagues, even those who are not specialists in the same field, to apply a set of agreed-upon standards to a body of scholarly work. Using

Table 3.1. Regarding *Teaching*, Which of the Following Methods of Evaluation Are Generally Used at Your Institution for Purposes of Promotion and Tenure?

	CURRENTLY IN GENERAL USE	NOT IN GENERAL USE BUT UNDER CONSIDERATION	NOT IN GENERAL USE AND NOT UNDER CONSIDERATION AT THIS TIME
a. Systematic student evaluations of classroom teaching	98%	2%	0%
b. Self-evaluation or personal statement	82	12	5
c. Peer review of syllabi, examinations, and other teaching materials	62	29	8
d. Peer review of classroom teaching	58	33	9
e. Evidence of continuing student interest (i.e., majors, course enrollment)	34	26	37
f. Alumni opinions	31	29	38
g. Student evaluations of advising	24	42	31
h. Evidence of student achievement	24	41	33
i. Evidence of the impact of teaching on research	15	29	51
j. Evidence of the impact of teaching on applied scholarship	14	29	51

Source: The Carnegie Foundation for the Advancement of Teaching, National Survey on the Reexamination of Faculty Roles and Rewards, 1994.

Table 3.2. Regarding *Research*, Which of the Following Methods of Evaluation Are Generally Used in Faculty Evaluation at Your Institution?

	CURRENTLY IN GENERAL USE	NOT IN GENERAL USE BUT UNDER CONSIDERATION	NOT IN GENERAL USE AND NOT UNDER CONSIDERATION AT THIS TIME
a. Securing a self-evaluation or personal statement	77%	9%	11%
b. Securing judgments by colleagues *within* the institution	73	11	15
c. Counting numbers of publications and presentations, weighted by type	54	8	37
d. Asking reviewers to use specific qualitative criteria in their evaluations	44	16	37
e. Evidence of a research project's impact on teaching	42	26	27
f. Securing judgments by *outside* scholars	39	17	43
g. Evidence of student participation in a research project	37	23	35
h. Evidence of a research project's impact on applied scholarship	34	22	37

Source: The Carnegie Foundation for the Advancement of Teaching, National Survey on the Reexamination of Faculty Roles and Rewards, 1994.

Table 3.3. Regarding *Applied Scholarship* (Outreach), Which of the Following Methods of Evaluation Are Generally Used at Your Institution for Purposes of Promotion and Tenure?

	CURRENTLY IN GENERAL USE	NOT IN GENERAL USE BUT UNDER CONSIDERATION	NOT IN GENERAL USE AND NOT UNDER CONSIDERATION AT THIS TIME
a. Self-evaluation or personal statement	74%	10%	13%
b. Client or user evaluation	35	23	38
c. Evidence of student participation in a project	32	26	37
d. Evidence of the impact of applied scholarship on teaching	30	26	38
e. Evaluations of the project by specialists	23	22	50
f. Evidence of the impact of applied scholarship on future research	20	24	48

Source: The Carnegie Foundation for the Advancement of Teaching, National Survey on the Reexamination of Faculty Roles and Rewards, 1994.

the standards we have proposed, documentation should address the following questions on a project-by-project basis, and ultimately, across the board:

- Are the scholar's goals clear?
- Has the scholar prepared adequately for the project?
- Does the scholar use appropriate methods?
- Does the scholar obtain significant results and communicate effectively?
- Does the scholar engage in reflective critique?

To answer these questions, we propose that a "professional profile" become part of the evaluation process. Such a profile might have three principal parts. First, to be fair, it would begin with a *statement of responsibilities* for the period under review, expectations set personally by the scholar or incorporated into a contract negotiated with the institution. Second, for breadth, a *biographical sketch* would list the scholar's achievements in the relevant areas of scholarly work. Third, for depth, *selected samples* of the scholar's best work would be documented to the standards by a reflective essay and by rich and varied materials.

Statement of Responsibilities

A statement of responsibilities should begin the professional profile by defining what the scholar had hoped or agreed to accomplish. This statement establishes a basis for judging the scholar's work. A thoughtful report on faculty roles and rewards at Northeastern University defines the issue: "Workload assignments give one very fundamental message about how . . . faculty members should balance their roles."[10]

It is essential in faculty evaluation to weigh carefully the commitments that the scholar has made. If, for instance, a scholar has heavy teaching responsibilities, the institution cannot reasonably expect him or her to have accomplished as much in discovery, integration, or applied scholarship as those who teach fewer hours.

This statement might conclude with the scholar's reflections on the overall pattern of his or her work and future plans. How do the person's scholarly activities fit together, for example, and what would the scholar like to accomplish in the next three to five years? How does the scholar's work help meet departmental and institutional needs?

Biographical Sketch

Evidence of scholarly accomplishment commensurate with one's responsibilities comes next in the professional profile. A biographical sketch depicts the scope and productivity of a scholar's activities in the quantitative sense of the term.

Documentation of teaching effectiveness, for instance, requires broad evidence of the sort that lends itself to a biographical sketch. In fact, many colleges and universities already follow this practice. Faculty at the University of Kentucky, for example, must submit a list of all courses taught for the period under review, including number of students enrolled and a brief description of each course, syllabi, and quantitative and qualitative summaries of student evaluations. The university also requests a brief reflective statement giving "whatever information may be necessary to provide colleagues with a context for interpreting and understanding the other evaluative information."[11]

The School of Humanities and Social Sciences at Rensselaer Polytechnic Institute asks faculty to maintain a current biographical sketch concerning nine areas of performance, which would seem to assure attention to breadth. One of these areas is teaching, and it includes a list of the number and title of each course taught, the enrollments, information on student thesis supervision, and information on course and curriculum development. The publications area includes monographs and chapters in edited volumes, articles and abstracts, letters of correspondence, book reviews in journals, and other publications such as major research reports. For such fields as architecture, provisions are made to take note of buildings, planning projects, renderings, and models.

The Rensselaer biography continues with "research grants and contracts," the category for listing proposals approved, funded, or pending as well as a narrative statement of current research interests. "Editorship of journals, reviews of manuscripts, books, and research proposals" is followed by "service to the university," a place to take note of committee work and administrative duties, student advising and counseling, professional society activities, and community and public service. Other categories in the Rensselaer sketch are "professional and public lectures," "honors and awards," "sabbatical leaves, off-campus study programs, and foreign professional travel," and "other activities," which would be the place to list such roles as consulting and serving as an expert witness.[12]

Clearly, the biographical sketch, properly structured, can provide a detailed picture of one's professional work. It also speaks to the kinds of scholarly activity valued by a particular institution; therefore, the emphasis on certain activities might vary from place to place.

Selected Samples of Scholarly Work

Documentation in depth cannot and should not involve the entire output of a scholar's efforts. A reflective essay, accompanied by rich and varied materials, should focus on selected samples of the scholar's best work.

A project of discovery, for example, would be represented by a limited number of publications or presentations. Integrative or applied efforts would be selected only when part of a larger intellectual project. As Ernest Lynton has argued, "for faculty evaluation, a much clearer distinction needs to be made between the minor professional outreach activities in which a faculty member might be engaged, and the specific, substantive projects that can serve as principal units of assessment."[13]

The selective documentation that allows for the evaluation of teaching as an *intellectual* project differs from the routine documentation necessary to ensure that students are served well. At the precollegiate level, for instance, the pioneering Stanford Teacher's Assessment Project concluded that teachers' unique styles were most effectively illustrated through samples of their best work. Similar arguments have been made for college and university teaching.[14] Ultimately, the projects selected for full documentation should be substantial enough to sustain judgment by the same standards as other kinds of scholarly work.

A reflective essay would introduce the projects selected, addressing their goals, preparation, methods, and results; presentation of the project; and self-critique and development. This is the place to highlight what was special about the project and, as Larry Braskamp and John Ory suggest, "to display the thinking behind the work."[15]

In teaching, for example, one recent winner in The Carnegie Foundation for the Advancement of Teaching U.S. Professors of the Year Program used his statement to emphasize his efforts to "wire" philosophy students in his New England classroom with students in a colleague's seminar in Norway. He explained how this exercise in the use of technology was connected with his exploration of the philosophical dimensions of new electronic communication. Another winner focused on the ways in which his literature courses had been enriched by his acting career in regional theater. His experiences on the stage had convinced him of the usefulness of "blocking" the positions of the characters when teaching about Renaissance drama, for example. A third winner featured her efforts to make mathematics come alive outside the traditional classroom by organizing a weekly colloquium for faculty and students and by training students for mathematical competitions. Explanations of the kind offered by these scholars could be included in a reflective essay for faculty evaluation as well as for award competitions.

The reflective essay—addressing the whats, hows, and whys of one's projects—is important, but not enough in itself. Applied to the same grid of standards, documentary evidence should also be provided to ensure the candidate's "accuracy in reporting"[16] and to help make the case for the quality of the selected work. A scholar highlighting a particular course as an example of his or her best teaching might bring together the course syllabus and examples of class materials, assignments, and examinations as evidence of the goals, preparation, and methods of teaching. Samples of student work could attest to the significance of results, and papers or publications can indicate the candidate's efforts at presentation. The scholar could demonstrate attention to reflective critique by showing how student evaluations of the class were taken into consideration.

In addition, statements from students who have gone on to graduate study or employment can offer special insights into the nature of a professor's impact. A graduate of a community college, writing in support of his former biology professor, recalled the time they collaboratively prepared an application for a grant for an undergraduate research fellowship. "For many weeks," the student wrote "we spent long nights together trying to decipher research papers, to understand concepts, and to define an important issue. . . . Ultimately, my application was successful and I was able to complete three productive research stints, resulting in subsequent publications of the work." Such letters add valuable personal testimony about a scholar's teaching methods and interaction with students.

Candidates might also ask colleagues with whom they have collaborated to comment on the goals, preparation, and methods by which the candidate approached important teaching responsibilities. Faculty who have benefited from discussions of teaching with the candidate may add to the picture of his or her effectiveness of presentation. A letter of recommendation, for example, might emphasize a scholar's commitment to mentoring colleagues. We saw one such letter that was written on behalf of someone whose approach to the teaching of writing to underprepared students had influenced colleagues throughout a multicampus urban university. In the same vein, scholars who mentor other faculty or who bring colleagues new ideas about teaching can be recognized for extending the lessons of teaching beyond the classroom.

Some evidence is best gathered not by the professor under review but by the department chair or committee head. The representative of the department or the committee can solicit student evaluations of classroom teaching and peer review statements. A department chair also may be the best person to describe how the candidate's teaching fits into the undergraduate or graduate program and how it relates to services to students for which the department is responsible.

Virtually all colleges and universities now survey students for their reactions to classroom teaching. In the 1992 Carnegie Foundation international survey of college and university faculty in fourteen countries, 91 percent of American professors reported that their teaching was regularly evaluated by students.[17] Sweden was the only country in which a higher percentage of respondents said that students regularly evaluated teaching. Yet, while most faculty (73 percent in the United States) agreed that student opinions should be used in evaluating teaching effectiveness, the same proportion also agreed that their institutions needed better ways of evaluating teaching performance. This attitude probably reflects a conviction that students should not be the only or principal sources of evidence about teaching effectiveness. It also may indicate faculty concern about how student opinion is tapped and how it is used. In any event, the need for "better ways to evaluate teaching performance" is felt keenly throughout the world. In ten of the fourteen countries surveyed, at least two-thirds of the faculty members said that their institutions needed such improvement in evaluation.

When student rating forms became common during the 1960s and 1970s, many faculty wondered whether the special care that they tried to bring to the act of teaching could be reflected fairly in the ratings. The instruments, even properly designed, provide good evidence only if used well. John Centra offered sensible guidelines for good practice in the use of evaluations. They include examining several sets of evaluation results for each professor for patterns or trends; making sure that a sufficient number of students evaluate each course; considering course characteristics and comparative data when interpreting results; relying primarily on global or summary items (rather than questions about specific aspects of the scholar's teaching) for purposes of personnel decisions; and not overestimating the importance of small differences in scores.[18]

Educators have sought for years to bring colleagues and peers more systematically into the review of teaching. Faculty are understandably concerned about bias when it comes to classroom visits and even to reviews of materials. But their fears can be allayed if colleagues who are conducting the evaluation also are meaningfully engaged in other ways. Colleagues are, after all, best situated to evaluate the course objectives, format, content, and grading policies of their peers, and they can win trust and be more helpful when expectations and understandings of the criteria for good teaching are public and shared. The American Association of Higher Education's innovative project on the peer review of teaching has sought to make teaching the subject of regular collegial exchange. Hutchings, director of the AAHE Teaching Initiative, said, "What's needed are ways for faculty to be professional colleagues to one another in teaching as they are in research."[19]

The hope that some form of peer review might be brought to bear on teaching is sparking experimentation throughout higher education. The University of Washington mandated the evaluation of teaching effectiveness by colleagues starting in 1987, annually for assistant professors and at least once every three years for associate and full professors. Departments were asked to develop their own particular peer review programs using, for example, class visits by colleagues and peer evaluation of teaching materials, student evaluations, and student performance.[20] The University of Washington is not alone. The Carnegie Foundation's 1994 National Survey on the Reexamination of Faculty Roles and Rewards found that peer review of classroom teaching was in place at 58 percent of colleges and under consideration at an additional 33 percent. Peer reviews of syllabi, examinations, and other teaching materials were already used at 62 percent of colleges and universities and under consideration at another 29 percent (Table 3.1).

In the end, the value of colleagues as sources for evidence about teaching effectiveness depends not only on their knowledge of the subject and their familiarity with the candidate's work as a teacher but also on the questions they ask. Their questions should relate clearly and powerfully to the standards of quality that the committee will use in its deliberations.

The selected samples needed to document the scholarship of integration and the scholarship of application are not fundamentally different from those required to document the scholarship of teaching. A reflective essay can introduce examples of best work, and the scholar can document the projects with appropriate materials, addressing the same standards in regard to goals, preparation, methods, results, presentation, and critique. The actual materials submitted to depict the project would vary. Documentation for a museum exhibit, for example, would differ from that for an interdisciplinary conference the scholar had organized; a consulting project with industry would produce different kinds of materials than collaboration with a local school. Each type of project would also be illuminated by a somewhat different mix of evaluators: peers or specialists knowledgeable about the kind of project under review—collaborators, clients, and beneficiaries of various kinds.

Consider the application of knowledge to clinical problems, a principal responsibility for many professional school faculty, especially in health care and in education. Duquesne University said of these clinical professors, "Because the great majority of their faculty responsibilities occur in the didactic and clinical teaching domain, their scholarly effort will focus upon remaining abreast of the latest methods of delivery of service in their area of specialty."[21] Harvard University Medical School has developed evaluative criteria that recognize the applied dimensions of clinical scholarship. For these faculty, Harvard looks for evidence of a high level of competence in a clinical area, using and developing innovative approaches, technologies, instrumentation, or systems of patient care.[22] Best work in this area could be documented to the same standards and with the same rich and varied materials as other types of scholarly work.

Finally, a few words about the consequences for documentation when the scholarship of discovery is held to the same standards as other types of scholarship. In many cases, a scholar's research is best represented by peer-reviewed publications and standard indicators of its reception in the scholarly community: grants, book reviews, awards, invitations to speak, and the like. But the reflective essay that we propose would pay more attention to the context and process of the project, to help colleagues, especially those in other fields, understand the goals guiding the work, the preparation, the choice of methods, the significance of results, the various ways in which the findings have been presented, and the steps taken for reflection and critique. The scholar may offer further documentation to support these points if he or she believes it will help make the case. The candidate or the committee, in seeking external reviews, should of course be sure to inform reviewers of the criteria by which the candidate's work will be judged.

Documentation describing the rationale of scholarly projects and how they are undertaken may encourage more risk taking and experimentation than traditional documentation focused on outcomes, not only in discovery but in integrative and applied work and in teaching as well. When the reasoning behind a project is considered important, scholars can draw attention to innovative explorations of high promise that may not yet have been implemented or completed but that nevertheless meet many of the standards of good scholarship.

Good documentation is dynamic, producing not merely a snapshot but a moving picture of the why as well as the what, the process as well as the products of scholarly work. The standards we have proposed illustrate this process and capture the reasoning and reflection shared by scholarship of different kinds. Documentation that addresses these standards familiarizes campus colleagues with the contexts surrounding the scholarly projects they are asked to review. It provides colleagues with a way of seeing scholarship whole, from several points of view, so that they can come to their own professional judgment on the quality of the work.

Documentation should place scholarly work in perspective. The scholar presents, explains, and interprets his or her best work for those who will review it, in the process renewing his or her own reflective critique. Documentation also opens doors for dialogue in departments, professional schools, and campuswide forums. The faculty will grow more conversant with the range of scholarship performed by colleagues in their own and other disciplines as they discuss documentation and the kinds of evidence needed to make the best case for any piece of work. It may not always be a peaceable kingdom: the lion may not lie down with the lamb. But this approach has the potential to make the campus a more just community, where varying contributions to the institution's mission are better understood and more fairly honored once they are made public and evaluated by the highest standards to which scholars can aspire.

CHAPTER FOUR

Trusting the Process

T HE INTRODUCTION of new definitions and new standards of scholarship
heightens the need to ensure that faculty evaluation is a trustworthy
process. The campus community must be confident that the institution
honors the range of scholarship that supports its mission and that appropriate
standards are in fact used. The commitment of colleagues to a conscientious
application of the standards is key. As one senior professor with long experience
on his institution's promotion and tenure committee put it, "In the end, faculty
must believe that they will be treated fairly. It's far more important to have a climate of trust than well-defined standards, as important as they may be."

A process that broadens definitions of scholarship, adheres to qualitative
standards, and uses rich documentation enhances trust. Clearly, however, these
same innovations widen the scope of judgment in evaluation. Broader definitions of scholarship and richer documentation introduce new kinds of work and
evidence into the process. Therefore, a framework of trust must buttress this
process so that faculty feel free to engage in a wide range of scholarly activities.
Only then can higher education institutions meet their missions of research,
teaching, and service through applied and integrative scholarly work.

Given the importance of evaluation to both individual scholars and their institutions, faculty should come to view the process as a collaboration involving each
segment of the academic community: students, through the faculty rating forms
they submit; faculty, through the committees in which they participate; deans,
provosts, and presidents, through the policies they carry out; and trustees,

through the policies they ratify. As a collaborative project, it follows, faculty evaluation should then be subject to the same standards proposed in this report for assessing scholarship itself.

Understood in this way, successful evaluation would be a process with *clear goals* for institutional and individual performance and *adequate preparation* for evaluators and candidates. *Appropriate methods* would be used, and *significant results* would advance the institution and individuals toward their goals. The process would be *effectively presented* and discussed as openly as possible in public forums. Finally, *reflective critique* would keep evaluation flexible and open to improvement over time.

Goals

Creating a climate of trust on campus requires a sense of common purpose among faculty and administrative leaders. The process of evaluation should embody goals that leave no doubt about expectations for institutional and individual performance.

Unfortunately, faculty over the last generation have received mixed messages about what work counts, leading to anxiety about the trustworthiness of the process. During this period, institutions maintained an official commitment to their traditional missions of teaching, research, and service. But many colleges and universities made deliberate efforts to enhance their reputations by recruiting faculty who showed promise of special achievement in research and, in effect, raised publication requirements. These shifting standards for employment and advancement were not always explicitly communicated nor consistently applied, engendering a climate of suspicion among faculty members who were left wondering about institutional goals.

A generation gap developed in many departments between faculty hired before and after new expectations for research productivity began to take effect. Disparities also widened between faculty from departments with heavy teaching loads and/or clinical responsibilities and colleagues from departments with a clearer focus on research.[1] And at many newly research-intensive institutions, faculty and administrators blamed each other for the undervaluation of teaching. A 1990 survey by Syracuse University's Center for Instructional Development concluded that faculty and administrators at research universities each viewed themselves as assigning more relative importance to teaching than was ascribed to them by others.[2]

Now, as they move to restore balance among faculty roles, colleges and universities should pay special attention to institutional missions and implications for the objectives of scholarly work. The most important step may be the first: building what Antioch University Chancellor Alan Guskin calls "a working consensus around a vision of the institution's future."[3] This usually starts with the recognition by administrative and faculty leaders of an urgent need to redefine and realign institutional missions and professors' work. Building the necessary consensus involves bringing as many people as possible into the conversation. Faculty are more trusting of a system in which they play a consequential role in shaping the model and in working out ways for their various departments to contribute to the goals.

No doubt as most institutions continue to voice support for the traditional missions of teaching, research, and service, many will want to consider whether to fill a particular niche. This may be especially important for colleges and universities that have never fit comfortably within either the research university model or the liberal arts college design. For example, we have talked to provosts from a group of universities that wish to serve their host cities better by enhancing the importance of service learning for students and applied scholarship for the professoriate. Likewise, the Associated New American Colleges, a group of private comprehensive colleges and universities, hopes to create at these schools an "ethos of community engagement," in which the scholarship of integration and the scholarship of application would occupy privileged positions.[4]

Colleges that have remained primarily teaching institutions might also ask new questions about the relationship between institutional mission and faculty work. Our inquiries concerning changes in systems of faculty roles and rewards found that many institutions are, in fact, exploring ways to improve the scholarship of teaching on their campuses. The interim president of Plymouth (New Hampshire) State College, for example, told us that the institution had "clarified and expanded the statement of our requirements to emphasize our theme of student success and involvement in learning."[5]

At doctoral and research institutions, too, the different divisions, including the professional schools, are specifying their own goals for faculty scholarship. The New School for Social Research, for example, explained that it has been engaged "in the endeavor to re-examine the processes and policies guiding faculty roles and rewards in the seven quite distinctive divisions of the university." In the New School's Graduate Faculty of Political and Social Sciences, "a high tenure standard with regard to scholarly publications was reaffirmed." But at the Parsons School of Design, which offers the largest portion of the New School's undergraduate degrees, "artistic accomplishment and demonstrated capacity to work effectively with students in the various arts and design fields are . . . more important . . . than scholarly publication."[6]

Departmental goals should relate closely to those of the larger institution, although expectations for faculty scholarship certainly vary among departments. For example, biochemistry and classics may differ in the size of classes; in the funding and equipment needed for an active program of discovery; and also in opportunities for application, interdisciplinary study, and public scholarship.

In the end, nothing assumes greater importance in faculty evaluation than the need to clarify goals for individual performance. The American Association of University Professors pointed out that it is a basic tenet of good practice to have a written agreement concerning "the precise terms and conditions of every appointment."[7] Such agreements, periodically renewed, can guide faculty effort toward departmental and institutional goals. A department might wish to encourage a faculty member's interest in developing a new area of expertise: a professor of literature moving into the study of popular film, or a professor of economics gravitating to the economics of environmental conservation. A department might also wish to encourage a faculty member's desire to develop different types of scholarly work. Indeed, in *Scholarship Reconsidered,* we proposed that all institutions establish creativity contracts, an arrangement in which faculty members define their professional goals for a three-to-five-year period, possibly shifting from one principal scholarly focus to another.

Preparation

With broader definitions of scholarship in place, the campus community must prepare itself to evaluate a wider range of scholarly work. Administrative leaders and faculty should agree on appropriate standards and documentation; training should be provided for chairpersons and committee members; and scholars facing evaluation should receive the guidance they need.

At most colleges and universities, the candidate's departmental colleagues make the first and most important evaluations. But for critical decisions concerning tenure and promotion, the department's recommendation is usually reviewed by a committee of faculty from other fields, by academic administrators, by the president, and even by the governing board. At some institutions, as Max E. Pierson explained, "The anomaly is that the people with the greatest power to retain or promote you are the furthest removed and least likely to be familiar with your work."[8] How can faculty be sure that all these people are adequately prepared to contribute to the process?

Confidence requires, in the first place, broad understanding and consensus regarding the standards applied to faculty work. The standards we suggest can form a basis for discussions that should take place as each campus arrives at its own formulation of a common language for evaluating the various kinds of scholarship. This campuswide formulation can then provide a framework for more explicit discussions among scholars in specific disciplines and professional fields. It is critical, however, to keep discussions flowing across departmental boundaries.

Faculty also need assurance that new standards have the unqualified support of the deans, provost, and president. Members of the faculty at an institution in

The Carnegie Foundation's study of architecture education stressed the need that they felt, with each change of provost, to "educate" the new administrator in the particulars of scholarship by design-oriented professors. With good campus preparation, such as that sought by these academic architects, dramatic reversals of recommendations by faculty committees over issues of merit would be less apt to occur. Indeed, nothing demoralizes a campus more quickly than administrative action based on ideas about scholarship that differ from those of the faculty. As Raoul Arreola commented in regard to the development of comprehensive faculty evaluation systems, "Of the two threats to success—administrator apathy and faculty resistance—administrator apathy is the more deadly. If the administration is apathetic toward, or actively against, the whole program, *it will not succeed.*"[9]

Beyond the preparation provided by campus, school, or departmental conversations, training sessions should be held for members of evaluation committees to review guidelines for documenting and evaluating scholarly work. After all, when definitions of scholarship are broadened, some scholars will submit work that balances discovery, integration, application, and teaching in unusual ways. Committees must learn how to weigh this work in accord with individual contracts; they may have to examine unusual documents, listen to new kinds of referees, and discuss how to apply qualitative standards to unfamiliar scholarly work.

Candidates themselves need adequate preparation so that they understand which materials to present to committees. Unfortunately, many newly hired junior faculty members get next to no formal guidance in preparing for evaluation. We have heard of candidates who relied solely on advice from the departmental secretary and word-of-mouth among friends. In fact, surveys indicate that "most individuals who go through the process for attaining promotion and tenure do so without ever having received specific, sufficient information about the expectations involved."[10]

The scholar should learn about the review process: how often, how formal, and how important the various reviews may be; the type of documentation that is expected, so that it can be assembled thoughtfully over time; the steps the committee follows; the criteria that are used to assess the quality of one's scholarly work; and the relative weighting of various activities.[11]

If evaluation is seen as a community project, no one—junior or senior faculty—should have to face these questions alone. The same proposals for making teaching and other types of scholarship "community property" might be adapted or broadened so as to apply to the process for promotion and tenure. Russell Edgerton and his colleagues, for instance, urge those experimenting with teaching portfolios to encourage collaboration, suggesting such possibilities as buddy systems, mentors, and a library of portfolio collections that could be retained in the department[12]—ideas that might all be helpful to faculty preparing for full-scale performance reviews. We are aware of an apprentice program instituted to improve the evaluation process after a litigated tenure dispute: George LaNoue and Barbara Lee observed that in a few departments at the University of Connecticut all junior faculty members were required "to serve on the department's tenure and promotion review committee during their second year so that they will understand the standards and process that will be used when they themselves are candidates for tenure."[13]

Good mentoring is surely the best preparation for faculty evaluation, although it is the hardest to write into the rules. A good mentor can coach a scholar through the major decisions that he or she must make in the probationary years, indeed, throughout a career. Young scholars in particular make many choices about when to pursue the various strands of their research, which courses to design or teach, what applied work or public scholarship to undertake. A good mentor has an eye for the contributions that rate highest with the department or program and can also advise a young scholar about the administrative and committee work that is expected of him or her. Mentoring may prove especially important for minority and female faculty, who frequently face extra pressures in the course of their careers.

Methods

Attempts to broaden scholarship have their greatest chance for success when the process of evaluation uses methods that institutionalize expectations concerning the breadth and quality of scholarship.

A scholar's trust in evaluation depends on what he or she believes is going on behind closed doors. Predictable methods should produce no surprises. Annual reviews for junior faculty should not amount to routine exercises. Instead, the evaluation should comment helpfully on progress toward reappointment and tenure. Likewise, a midcourse review for probationary faculty should function as a dress rehearsal for the tenure decision that looms on the horizon. The tenure decision itself should prepare a scholar for promotion reviews to follow and, in a growing number of institutions, for periodic post-tenure reviews. Most important, reviews each step of the way should be connected to each other and thus bolster confidence in the system.

The more disciplined the methods of evaluating scholarship, the less room scholars have for concern that their work will be unfairly judged. Reviewers should assess quality according to the published standards, carefully balancing the sources of information about the scholar's major areas of work. This is especially important in regard to outside letters of support. A Northwestern University report notes: "Since scholars at other institutions do not necessarily have information concerning a colleague's classroom performance at Northwestern, teaching performance is generally 'invisible' outside the university. In a promotion and tenure process that gives heavy weight to 'outside' letters, it is almost inevitable that teaching will receive less weight than research in this crucial part of the reward system."[14]

An institution can also show its seriousness of purpose in regard to recognizing a broader range of scholarship through thoughtful composition of evaluation committees. It is not always possible nor even desirable to limit committees to what the Quakers call "weighty brethren," those members of the community whose senior standing gives them respect. The brothers and sisters who do serve as members of review committees should have varied backgrounds and interests so as to avoid any narrow orthodoxy and to foster receptivity to scholarship in all its varied forms. Indeed, at Pennsylvania State University, it has been recommended that at "campus, department, college, and University levels, promotion and tenure committees should be composed of *both* pedagogically and research oriented scholars."[15]

Results

A trustworthy process of evaluation leads to the intellectual growth of individual faculty and enables the institution to fulfill its collective goals. The results of evaluation should therefore strengthen the academic community by assuring the institution of a well-qualified professoriate, while also serving needs for professional development.

Colleges and universities have much at stake in the evaluation of faculty scholarship. Institutional missions are more than abstract ideals. The success of the institution depends ultimately on the quality of the scholars it attracts and retains. Indeed, as the University of California's landmark *Report of the Universitywide Task Force on Faculty Rewards* states, ". . . the University's success in accomplishing its mission depends on the selection and advancement of its faculty. The criteria for appointment and promotion of faculty are critically important to ensure the continuing vitality of the University."[16]

Of course, the results of assessment are crucial to the scholars themselves. Professors judge the results of faculty evaluation partly on the basis of whether their scholarly opportunities were expanded or constrained. Even those who gain tenure or promotion may grade poorly a system that has diverted their effort from important professional goals, or that has not encouraged enough attention to the work they have actually been asked to do. A broader definition of scholarship supported through evaluation would reduce such dissonance and widen horizons.

Evaluation makes faculty take time out from their ongoing work to record and document their achievements. Scholars will judge the system on the basis

TRUSTING THE PROCESS 57

of whether documentation was just a make-work task, or whether it actually repaid the effort by inspiring learning and reflection. Routine documentation leads to just that: a routine collection of publications and student evaluation results. A good system of rich and varied documentation, however, can encourage faculty to keep an eye on their different projects over time, seeking new types and sources of evidence that speak to goals, preparation, methods, significance, presentation, and critique.

Finally, evaluation also provides scholars with feedback from their colleagues about the quality of their work. Faculty will judge the process, then, partly in terms of the helpfulness of the critique it provides. When this feedback is limited to yea or nay, a real opportunity for development may be lost. In a good system of evaluation, colleagues stay in touch with the scholar throughout the process and report on the balance and quality of the full range of his or her work. One can imagine a report that notes weaknesses and strengths based on standards such as those we have suggested. As the evaluation proceeds, for example, a scholar might learn that his or her goals and preparation strike evaluators as strong across the board, but that more attention should be paid to methods of teaching or to the presentation of applied work.

Recommendations of this kind can form the basis for informal discussions with the chairperson or dean. When the process fails and scholars fear they have been unfairly judged, the system should allow scholars the chance to appeal. These procedures should follow guidelines suggested by the American Association of University Professors and provide legal safeguards to ensure the scholar's rights. John Centra noted that due-process considerations suggest that a formal hearing presided over by an impartial person should be available.[17] But just as important, such cases should alert the campus to issues of particular vulnerability so that the process does not fail in the same way again.

The sad history of litigation in tenure disputes clearly shows that an evaluation process that is not trusted can exacerbate divisions between junior and senior faculty, women and men, minorities and nonminorities, science and humanities departments, liberal arts and professional schools, faculty and administrators. When it works well, though, faculty evaluation brings people into common purpose, bridging the boundaries that too often separate academic lives. That common purpose, of course, is to build a strong and vital faculty that can help the institution meet its most important goals.

Presentation

Faculty evaluation can foster trust by operating as openly as possible, allowing for the presentation of as much of the process as practical to the scrutiny of audiences both within and beyond the academy.

We realize that the need to present the process openly must be balanced with an equally compelling obligation to respect confidentiality. On the one hand, some argue that an absence of confidentiality would discourage the candor of committee members and outside evaluators. On the other hand, some maintain that records should be open in order to win trust by demonstrating an absence of bias.[18] As Leslie Francis, then associate secretary for the American Association of University Professors, once put it: "You're weighing two good principles against each other—the right to privacy and the right to know. You want to protect the review process, and at the same time you don't want to allow unfair discrimination."[19]

Though faculty evaluation for purposes of reappointment, tenure, and promotion necessarily takes place in private, it can, like teaching, raise general issues that should become community property through open exchange. Discussion about goals, preparation, methods, and results of evaluation should be ongoing. The more widespread the conversation, the better. Certainly, it will feed back into the process by educating administrators and faculty to be better committee members, and helping scholars fill their role as candidates, too.

The best faculty evaluation has a dimension that extends beyond any particular campus or university system. The Carnegie Foundation's 1994 Survey on Faculty Roles and Rewards found, for example, that 39 percent of four-year institutions currently seek judgments on faculty research by outside scholars. These specialists belong to larger, more diffuse, disciplinary and professional communities, where ideas about the kinds of work esteemed in particular subject areas are formed.

Colleges and universities can bolster support for a broader range of scholarship by a more public presentation of evaluation practices. Meetings of regional and national professional and disciplinary associations may provide forums for discussing the idea of a more inclusive approach to scholarship. These discussions can be further advanced on the pages of newsletters, magazines, journals, and even through e-mail, in order to reach a variety of scholarly audiences. In the long run, successful change in faculty roles and rewards depends on recognition that all types of scholarship can be evaluated by standards these larger communities share.

No process of faculty evaluation is complete unless it is also shared with those outside the academy. Public trust in colleges and universities cannot simply be assumed. It is no longer taken for granted that higher education fulfills its traditional missions. The academy is spending more effort defending its research mission and publicizing its teaching efforts. At the same time, it is finding that the professional service mission has more appeal now than previously. Public scholarship, too, needs more attention. Christopher Clausen, of Pennsylvania State University, noted that "another . . . factor that lowers the public recognition of American universities is the comparatively slight presence of regular faculty members, proportional to their vast numbers, in the cultural and intellectual life of the country."[20]

All parties to the academic enterprise can benefit by making public efforts to promote balance in faculty scholarship. As long as the nature and variety of faculty work is not well understood outside the academy, the working conditions under which scholarship thrives may well erode. The best argument will be results: showing that colleges and universities perform research responsibly, respect teaching, apply scholars' knowledge to important problems, and allow faculty to address nonacademic audiences, too. This is, we conclude, a time to engage policy makers and the public in conversations about quality in scholarship: the time that scholarship requires, how it can be recognized, and why it should be cultivated and passed on. As George Bernard Shaw once said, "The greatest problem in communication is the illusion it has been achieved."

Critique

As the American Association of University Professors points out, "a major responsibility of the institution is to recruit and retain the best qualified faculty within its goals and means."[21] Incisive critique identifies the factors in goals, preparation, methods, results, or presentation that can strengthen evaluation and aid an institution in attracting and holding those whom it would like to have on its faculty.

Ordinarily, institutions of all sorts—inside and outside higher education—lack systematic ways of engaging in self-adjustment. They need to scrutinize their practices and alter their procedures in the face of new realities. An orderly process of change can be aided immeasurably by asking: Where have we been and where are we headed?

A trustworthy process of faculty evaluation has continuity over time, while remaining flexible enough to accommodate special circumstances. Consider the issues that have figured in faculty evaluation in just the last two decades, issues involving gender, race, age, emerging fields, and new forms of scholarship. Each decision, as it is made, should be reviewed for the lessons it provides for future deliberations. An institution that displays sufficient confidence to examine itself cannot help but inspire the trust of its constituents, even in confronting difficult issues. The assessment of faculty evaluation is too important to be left to chance. It should be the result of careful, considered reflection.

The reflective critique that serves the institution as a whole can also provide valuable input for the individual. Through a creativity contract or some other flexible work plan, for instance, a faculty member may find it possible to focus for the next review period on developing new, updated courses, a new topic for research, or connections for applied scholarship with local schools or industry. In some cases, it may be possible to accommodate even more radical shifts.

A carefully monitored system of faculty evaluation can help maintain high standards while accommodating changes in the timing as well as the direction of academic careers. This flexibility may be especially important for younger women, whose desire to start a family is likely to coincide with their most pressure-filled academic years. Many institutions, in fact, agree to delay the tenure process for women in such situations, and some even consider innovative job-sharing arrangements in which two faculty members are considered separately for reappointment and tenure, while sharing the same position.[22] Broad definitions of scholarship and qualitative standards should facilitate these family-friendly policies, for younger faculty and also for older faculty with special responsibilities.

Any system of evaluation, whatever its purpose, must offer assurances of its trustworthiness each step of the way. Too much is at stake in evaluation to allow any one factor to undermine confidence in the entire process. Earlier in this report, we offered standards for evaluating faculty members; now we have recast those same standards so that they may be applied to evaluation itself. This is our suggestion for closing the circle. Ultimately, trustworthiness must permeate every aspect of higher education so as to enhance the reputation of the institution and the accomplishments of its scholars.

CHAPTER FIVE

The Qualities of a Scholar

C ERTAIN QUALITIES associated with a scholar's character are recognized by virtually all higher education institutions as consequential not only for the individual professor but for the entire community of scholars.

No statement of professional ethics, in fact, fails to mention that professors have special responsibilities to their disciplines, their students, their colleagues, and their institutions. And no college or university knowingly tolerates incompetence, neglect of duty, or scientific and scholarly misconduct among faculty members. But how many institutions, we wonder, have attempted to include among their criteria for faculty appointment and advancement a discussion of the personal qualities that they seek in a scholar?

We realize that even the suggestion of a connection between scholarship and personal qualities invites the possibility of bias. The academic appointment process through the years has, after all, included many reports of racial and gender bias as well as prejudicial judgments based on lifestyles and on political and religious orientations. During World War I, for example, Columbia University's president, Nicholas Murray Butler, dismissed some of the institution's most distinguished scholars and silenced others on the mere suspicion of their insufficient enthusiasm for the allied war effort.[1] And sometimes the faculty itself failed to uphold principles of tolerance. During the Cold War, in the early 1950s, Senator Joseph McCarthy's inquisition in search of communists gave pause to the deliberations of many a campus committee concerned about appointments and tenure.[2]

Linking scholarship to personal virtues certainly is not a new idea. For example, Assyriologist Anne Draffkorn Kilmer, of the University of California at Berkeley, said that the oldest known references to scholarship appear as inscriptions on forty-five-hundred-year-old Sumerian tablets. Scholarship in those ancient days referred to the literary culture that students had to master in order to become scribes. The tablets provide sobering admonitions to the young: "Day and night you must concentrate," they say. "You must sit still for scholarship, you must be humble."[3]

In the English-speaking world, the word *scholar* first appeared in the eleventh century, with a strong social component. *Scholarship,* according to the *Oxford English Dictionary,* was not seen as an isolated activity. A scholar of that day was typically a student who was training or had trained with a particular master. By the sixteenth century, the term applied to "one who has acquired learning in the 'Schools'" and meant "a learned or erudite person; especially one who is learned in the classical (i.e., Greek and Latin) languages and their literature."[4] In *Henry VIII,* William Shakespeare himself tried his hand at framing a definition of a scholar. Cardinal Woolsey, he wrote, "was a scholar and a ripe and good one. Exceeding wise, fair-spoken, and persuading"—human qualities we still admire in a scholar. Ralph Waldo Emerson, speaking in 1837 on "The American Scholar" at the Phi Beta Kappa Society at Cambridge, Massachusetts, said that "character is higher than intellect" for a scholar.[5] The scholar, Emerson proposed, required patience, bravery, and self-trust.[6]

In modern times, Wayne Booth, of the University of Chicago, has proposed in his influential article "The Scholar in Society" that at the very heart of a scholar's professional life are personal qualities that he calls "habits of rationality." These include courage, persistence, consideration, humility, and honesty—virtues, Booth argues, that are of great consequence in shaping the scholar's intellectual work and knowledge. Indeed, in Booth's view, the public role of the scholar is to serve as an exemplar of these virtues in society, to testify to the value of "shared reason" in public debate.[7]

Sir Eric Ashby, of Cambridge University, observes that while a university teacher belongs to an ancient and honorable profession, there is still a need for a "declared professional code of practice," a formulation resembling the Hippocratic oath to which physicians swear allegiance.[8] Ashby suggests that a scholar has an inner integrity, calling for a code that would not permit the scholar to hide some facts nor to consider race or religion or political party in assessing scholarship. The code would emphasize tolerance for other points of view and encourage both consent and dissent in debate.

A statement by the American Association of University Professors on professional ethics affirms intellectual honesty. The primary responsibility of professors to their subject, according to the AAUP, "is to seek and to state the truth as they see it."[9] And Talcott Parsons has written that competence in mastering knowledge and the techniques of its advancement were of supreme importance for those who claim the privilege of academic status, and with competence comes the obligation of integrity, a commitment to the values of the academic profession.[10] Edward Shils notes in his advice to appointment committees: ". . . the talent and the intellectual passion must be there already, although sometimes hidden from a casual eye."[11]

In considering the qualities of a scholar, we propose that three characteristics merit especial consideration: *integrity, perseverance,* and *courage.* To recognize these traits requires qualitative judgment, but this judgment need not be arbitrary when guided by a careful and impartial examination of the candidate.

Integrity

The foundation of academic life is integrity. The scholar's audience has to trust his or her work, ascribing integrity to it. In saying this, we note that integrity, and more specifically honesty, "implies truthfulness, fairness in dealing, and absence of fraud, deceit, and dissembling."[12]

In fact, scholarship cannot thrive without an atmosphere of trust. At the most basic level, scholars must be honest in reporting what they have done and what they have found. If a scholar claims to have performed certain experiments, engaged in a certain type of field work, interviewed certain people, or read certain documents, then that claim must be true. Likewise, the reported findings must be neither manufactured nor modified if a scholar claims that an experiment produced specific results, that an informant made particular statements, or that a document contained certain information.

The National Academy of Sciences uses its report *Responsible Science: Ensuring the Integrity of the Research Process* to discuss misconduct: fabrication, falsification, plagiarism, and other practices that can compromise the research process and endanger community trust. For example, with science and engineering fields in mind, the report cites "questionable research practices . . . that violate traditional values of the research enterprise," referring to those who would maintain "inadequate research records, especially for results that are published or are relied on by others," or refuse "to give peers reasonable access to unique research materials or data that support published papers," or use "inappropriate statistical or other methods of measurement to enhance the significance of research findings."[13] The credibility of scholarly inquiry requires integrity so that those whose words and ideas the scholar has used receive appropriate credit.

This is a prescription of long standing. Some cultures have idealized the scholar as a seeker of truth whose poverty is evidence of incorruptibility. Confucius is reported to have said, "The scholar who cherishes the love of comfort is not fit to be deemed a scholar."[14] Enticements are not limited to money and prestige. Shils argues that it is nearly as great a departure from duty for a teacher to present unsubstantiated opinion as established truth as it is to knowingly "put forward a false proposition as true. . . ."[15]

The right balance among values is not always easy to discern. Objectivity, for instance, has long been one of the hallmarks of integrity in scholarly inquiry, but objectivity was often understood to result from silencing one's preferences and beliefs. Today, though, the work of scholars gives increased attention to the influences of culture, gender, and class. The American Historical Association's "Statement on Standards of Professional Conduct" says it well: "Integrity . . . requires an awareness of one's own bias and a readiness to follow sound method and analysis wherever they may lead."[16] Booth has written that honest inquiry no longer requires us to "suppress our commitments" in the service of knowing, but to acknowledge and use them in the service of scholarly truth.[17] A scholar today upholds integrity by grappling openly and fairly with the sometimes contradictory claims of personal commitments and scholarly truths.

Fairness is another aspect of integrity, not only in inquiry but in the scholar's dealings with colleagues, students, and others involved in his or her work. Fairness requires such simple acts as taking care in publications to acknowledge financial support, sponsorship, and other kinds of assistance crucial to one's work. It also involves the presentation of one's own interpretations and conclusions in ways that keep open an examination of alternatives. And fairness, finally, revolves around a willingness to engage in such discussions. As the American Historical Association states: "The bond that grows out of lives committed to the study of history should be evident in the standards of civility that govern the conduct of historians in their relations with one another. The preeminent value of all intellectual communities is reasoned discourse—the continuous colloquy among historians of diverse points of view. A commitment to such discourse makes possible the fruitful exchange of views, opinions, and knowledge."[18] This is a statement that all scholars of integrity can embrace.

Perseverance

Institutions of higher education need scholars who persevere in their efforts. A young faculty member must give promise of a lifetime pursuit of scholarship. Colleges and universities cannot afford to waste valuable appointments on people who abandon scholarship once they win long-term employment. In his ideal university, Booth would have only one criterion for tenure and promotion: "Is this candidate *still curious,* still inquiring . . . and is it thus probable that at the age of forty, fifty, or sixty-six, he or she will still be vigorously inquiring?"[19]

Academic employment also demands a reasonable level of productivity. Students must be taught and advised. In some settings, productive participation in the scholarship of discovery or integration must be demonstrated by obtaining grants, presenting papers, and publishing books and articles. Applied work with patients or clients is sometimes required. Ability without productivity is unfulfilled potential. Because of the many demands on a professor's time, perseverance is essential.

We recognize that no tests can reveal who will persevere as a scholar. Those who attempt to take the measure of a scholar on this count must carefully weigh the evidence of past accomplishments. Is the person persistent? Does he or she see tasks to completion? C. Wright Mills, in his classic essay *On Intellectual Craftsmanship,* writes, "Scholarship is a choice of how to live as well as a choice of career." Intellectual workers, Mills continues, form their own character as they strive to perfect their craft. A scholar "constructs a character which has as its core the qualities of the good workman."[20]

For example, Ralph Tyler, a social scientist at the University of Chicago who was an influential authority on elementary and secondary education from the 1930s through the 1970s, owed his success to more than his considerable ability. Louis Rubin, writing of Tyler, said: "As with others marked by greatness, much of his talent resulted not from inherent gifts alone but from a portfolio of meticulously honed skills. Similarly, the exceptional length of his productivity stemmed neither from good fortune nor from special blessings, but rather from a systematically choreographed program to preserve his abilities. . . ."[21]

Good scholars, like good workmen, seek to perfect their craft over a lengthy period. As institutions of higher education increasingly engage in periodic reviews of those who already have tenure and look at others in connection with the renewal of long-term contracts, issues of perseverance must come to the fore. A committee should not be blinded by a brief blaze of glory at the beginning of a candidate's career. Veteran academics have had sufficient time to demonstrate the role of perseverance in their scholarship.

Courage

As a third attribute, a scholar must have the courage to risk disapproval in the name of candor. A scholar must possess the will to take on difficult or unpopular work that others avoid, transcending traditional ideas, rules, and patterns, and imagining new questions and problems.

A generation ago, this willingness to defy convention drove David Felten to pursue research on connections between the brain and the body's defenses against disease at a time when most scientists scoffed at the notion that the mind might send signals to the immune system; they believed that the immune system was under its own control. It took one of the grants that the MacArthur Foundation confers on highly talented individuals to give Felten the freedom to work in an important new scholarly area now known as psychoneuroimmunology.[22]

Thomas Ehrlich, president emeritus of Indiana University, entitled his book *The Courage to Inquire: Ideals and Realities in Higher Education,* calling courage to inquire, along with morality of reason, two of the most important attributes for flourishing at a university and for preparing for one's career. Ehrlich writes, "The courage to inquire is based on the faith that whatever the dangers inherent in the search for knowledge, those inherent in ignorance are far more ominous."[23]

Courage, it can be seen, may serve as the partner of originality. Those who dare to be different, who are bold enough to strike out in new directions, can produce transcendent scholarship. The capacity to exceed the known body of knowledge has been a constitutive value of science, for instance, since at least the onset of the eighteenth century.

Earlier, those who felt threatened by the originality of creative minds lashed out at challengers of the status quo. Galileo, for all his courage, won only the censure of the powerful in the early seventeenth century, when he turned his telescope on the heavens to confirm the theory of Copernicus that the earth is not the center of the universe but that it revolves around the sun.

What we see in the fruits of such courage are the seeds from which constructive public discourse sprouts. Scholars must possess the courage of their convictions so that their work ends up feeding the debates of the day. John Dewey argued in the 1920s that the scholar's role as expert does not excuse him or her from public debate, challenging scholars to "bring their intelligence and their findings into the public realm."[24]

A scholar must not confine his or her creative products to folders or computer files, however risky it may appear to enter the larger arena where ideas are critiqued and evaluated. Scholars must gain confidence that through their courage to move beyond the ordinary they can enrich and further theoretical knowledge, strengthen practical applications of knowledge, and demonstrate new ways of looking at the connecting points where different kinds of knowledge converge.

In short, the assessment of scholarship begins not with procedures but with ideals. This does not mean that a committee sitting down to evaluate a colleague would try to measure in quantitative terms the candidate's integrity, perseverance, and courage. Indeed, these qualities would lose their meaning if efforts were made to codify them formally.

Still, it is appropriate, we believe, to consider such qualities at the time that scholars are recruited or are reviewed for retention or tenure. In developing revised standards for faculty evaluation in the University of California, for instance, the Pister report recommends that "Evidence of a productive and creative mind should be sought" in the candidate's work.[25] And surely, we would add, if a committee confronts evidence that such key qualities of a scholar as integrity, perseverance, and courage are not present, the candidate's case would be seriously flawed.

These qualities of character should serve as reminders that good scholarship involves more than doing one's job well, as important as that is. Scholarship has a moral aspect that should figure in all of its dimensions: discovery, teaching, integration, and application.

Throughout this report, we have spoken of a need for clear goals, adequate preparation, appropriate methods, significant results, effective presentation, and reflective critique. We would like to see these standards embedded in qualities of character that ensure that evaluation and all activities connected to scholarship, including faculty development and self-enrichment, have a moral dimension. The university, for all of its concern about the intellect, must never lose sight of the ethical imperative by which it should be guided.

In concluding a report on evaluation with a discussion of character, we have no intention of putting forth romantic notions that have no basis in reality. But if higher education is to continue to help lead the nation, then surely its scholarly accomplishments, as laudable as they are, must be grounded in principles that speak to humankind's noblest aspects.

This report does not offer a formula. It does, however, provide a vocabulary for a thoroughgoing debate about the elements of faculty evaluation. Starting with the conception of the four forms of scholarship put forth in *Scholarship Reconsidered*, and continuing with this companion work, The Carnegie Foundation has sought to freshen the debate and give it focus. It is up to the scholars at each college or university to determine what is most appropriate for their institution to ensure that scholarship, in whatever form it may take, meets high standards of rigor and quality.

APPENDIX A
QUESTIONNAIRE FOR THE NATIONAL
SURVEY ON THE REEXAMINATION OF
FACULTY ROLES AND REWARDS, 1994

National Survey on the
Reexamination of Faculty Roles and Rewards

IN RESPONSE TO GROWING INTEREST in broadening the definition of scholarship, The Carnegie Foundation for the Advancement of Teaching is examining changes in the evaluation and reward of faculty work. Your careful response to this survey will contribute significantly to this study by helping map the scope and direction of such efforts.

We are most grateful for your participation.

1. In the past five years, has your college or university reexamined faculty roles and rewards? [Circle only one.]

   1 Yes, the review has been completed

   2 Yes, the review is still under way

   3 No, but we plan to initiate a review soon [Please skip to question 15.]

   4 No, we do not plan to initiate such a review in the near future [Please skip to question 15.]

2. What were the **most important** reasons for initiating the effort? [Circle those that apply.]

   1 Directive from the state legislature

   2 Directive from the system administration

   3 Directive from the governing board

   4 Leadership by this institution's president

   5 Leadership by other administrators

   6 Leadership by organized faculty

   7 Concern of a few key faculty members

   8 General dissatisfaction among faculty

   9 Models from other colleges or universities

   10 National reports on the state of higher education

   11 Other (please specify) _____

3. Please indicate the **primary** procedures you have used in conducting the review. [Circle those that apply.]

   1 A trustee review committee was formed

   2 An all-campus review committee was formed

   3 Each school or college within the institution has been responsible for reviewing its situation independently

   4 Each academic department has been responsible for reviewing its situation independently

   5 A chief academic or administrative officer has led campus discussions on faculty roles and rewards

   6 A series of campus sessions has been held to explore options

   7 Other (please specify) _____

4. Have any of the following issues been the focus of your review?

	YES	NO
a. Clarifying institutional mission	1	2
b. Redefining faculty roles (i.e., research/teaching/service)	1	2
c. Striking a balance between institutional mission and faculty rewards	1	2
d. Improving the balance of time and effort faculty spend on various tasks	1	2

5. Many institutions have sharpened the definition of faculty work. Do the following statements apply to your institution?

	YES	NO
a. The definition of scholarship is being broadened to include the full range of activities in which faculty are engaged.	1	2
b. The definition of teaching is being broadened to include activities such as curriculum development, advising, and conducting instructional and classroom research.	1	2
c. Applied scholarship (outreach) is being clearly distinguished from campus and community "citizenship" activity.	1	2
d. The role of faculty as campus citizens (service to the institution) is being clarified.	1	2

6. Have new methods of evaluating faculty been developed in the following areas?

	YES	NO
a. Teaching	1	2
b. Advising	1	2
c. Research	1	2
d. Creative work (i.e., art and design, dance, music)	1	2
e. Applied scholarship (outreach)	1	2
f. Service to the college or university (citizenship)	1	2
g. Service to the profession (citizenship)	1	2
h. Other (Please specify) _____	1	2

7. Regarding **research,** which of the following methods of evaluation are generally used in faculty evaluation at your institution? (By "generally," we mean use in most, if not all, departments and schools at a college or university.)

	YES, CURRENTLY IN GENERAL USE	NO, NOT IN GENERAL USE BUT UNDER CONSIDERATION	NO, NOT IN GENERAL USE AND NOT UNDER CONSIDERATION AT THIS TIME	DON'T KNOW
a. Counting numbers of publications and presentations, weighted by type	1	2	3	4
b. Asking reviewers to use specific qualitative criteria in their evaluations	1	2	3	4
c. Securing judgments by **outside** scholars	1	2	3	4
d. Securing judgments by colleagues **within** the institution	1	2	3	4
e. Securing a self-evaluation or personal statement	1	2	3	4
f. Evidence of student participation in a research project	1	2	3	4
g. Evidence of a research project's impact on teaching	1	2	3	4
h. Evidence of a research project's impact on applied scholarship	1	2	3	4

8. Regarding **teaching**, which of the following methods of evaluation are generally used at your institution for purposes of promotion and tenure? (By "generally," we mean use in most, if not all, departments and schools at a college or university.)

	YES, CURRENTLY IN GENERAL USE	NO, NOT IN GENERAL USE BUT UNDER CONSIDERATION	NO, NOT IN GENERAL USE AND NOT UNDER CONSIDERATION AT THIS TIME	DON'T KNOW
a. Self-evaluation or personal statement	1	2	3	4
b. Peer review of classroom teaching	1	2	3	4
c. Peer review of syllabi, examinations, and other teaching materials	1	2	3	4
d. Systematic student evaluations of classroom teaching	1	2	3	4
e. Student evaluations of advising	1	2	3	4
f. Evidence of student achievement	1	2	3	4
g. Evidence of continuing student interest (i.e., majors, course enrollment)	1	2	3	4
h. Alumni opinions	1	2	3	4
i. Evidence of the impact of teaching on research	1	2	3	4
j. Evidence of the impact of teaching on applied scholarship	1	2	3	4

9. Regarding **applied scholarship** (outreach), which of the following methods of evaluation are generally used at your institution for purposes of promotion and tenure? (By "generally," we mean use in most, if not all, departments and schools at a college or university.)

	YES, CURRENTLY IN GENERAL USE	NO, NOT IN GENERAL USE BUT UNDER CONSIDERATION	NO, NOT IN GENERAL USE AND NOT UNDER CONSIDERATION AT THIS TIME	DON'T KNOW
a. Self-evaluation or personal statement	1	2	3	4
b. Client or user evaluation	1	2	3	4
c. Evaluations of the project by specialists	1	2	3	4
d. Evidence of student participation in a project	1	2	3	4
e. Evidence of the impact of applied scholarship on teaching	1	2	3	4
f. Evidence of the impact of applied scholarship on future research	1	2	3	4

10. Thinking about your own situation, do the following faculty activities count more or less today—for purposes of faculty advancement—than they did five years ago?

	COUNT MORE TODAY THAN FIVE YEARS AGO	COUNT LESS TODAY THAN FIVE YEARS AGO	COUNT ABOUT THE SAME AS FIVE YEARS AGO	DON'T KNOW
a. Research	1	2	3	4
b. Teaching	1	2	3	4
c. Applied scholarship (outreach)	1	2	3	4
d. Service to the institution (citizenship)	1	2	3	4
e. Professional activity (national committees, etc.)	1	2	3	4

11. Many institutions have developed new ways to reward good teaching. Which of the following practices are now in place or are being considered at your institution?

	NOW IN PLACE	UNDER CONSIDERATION	NOT UNDER CONSIDERATION	DON'T KNOW
a. Merit increases for teaching excellence	1	2	3	4
b. Special awards for teaching excellence	1	2	3	4
c. Distinguished chairs for teaching excellence	1	2	3	4
d. Using distinguished teachers as mentors	1	2	3	4
e. Grants for course development	1	2	3	4
f. Release time for course development	1	2	3	4
g. Travel funds for teaching improvement purposes	1	2	3	4
h. Sabbaticals for teaching improvement purposes	1	2	3	4
i. A center for teaching improvement	1	2	3	4

12. Many tenure issues are now surfacing at colleges and universities. Have any of the following practices been implemented at your institution in the past five years?

	YES	NO, BUT UNDER CONSIDERATION	NO, NOT UNDER CONSIDERATION AT THIS TIME	DON'T KNOW/ NOT APPLICABLE
a. Changes in the criteria by which tenure is awarded	1	2	3	4
b. Regular post-tenure review of faculty	1	2	3	4
c. Negotiating the length of the probation period prior to tenure with individual faculty	1	2	3	4
d. Alternative contractual arrangements that do not include tenure	1	2	3	4
e. Abolishing tenure	1	2	3	4

13. In addition, have the following or any other ideas about faculty roles and rewards been introduced or considered at your institution?

	YES	NO, BUT UNDER CONSIDERATION	NO, NOT UNDER CONSIDERATION AT THIS TIME	DON'T KNOW/ NOT APPLICABLE
a. Encouraging faculty to shift their scholarly focus from time to time (concentrating on teaching, then research, for example)	1	2	3	4
b. Evaluating departmental performance, not just individuals	1	2	3	4
c. Working collaboratively with other institutions in developing new approaches in faculty roles and rewards	1	2	3	4
d. Other (please specify) _____	1	2	3	4

14. Has *Scholarship Reconsidered: Priorities of the Professoriate*, the 1990 Carnegie Foundation report, played a role in the discussion about faculty roles and rewards at your institution?

1 Yes
2 No

15. Finally, changes in **other** areas of institutional life have been introduced on many campuses. In the past five years, has your institution developed new approaches to any of the following?

	YES	NO	NOT APPLICABLE
a. General education for undergraduates (that part of the curriculum required of all or a large majority of students)	1	2	3
b. The quality of campus life (those events, services, and activities that make up a student's out-of-class experience in attending college)	1	2	3
c. Public and community service for students	1	2	3
d. Information technology for teaching and learning	1	2	3
e. Assessment of student learning	1	2	3

16. Please summarize anything else you would like to tell us about faculty evaluation at your institution.

If someone at your institution would be willing to discuss your policies with a representative of The Carnegie Foundation, who should be contacted?

Name: _____

Title: _____

Telephone number: _____

Address: _____

We would be most grateful to receive material from you which would give us further information about your institution's reexamination of faculty roles and rewards. If you have documents (task force reports, campus surveys, policy statements, and the like) that you would be willing to share with us, please send them to the address below.

Please return this questionnaire by November 21, 1994, to:

National Survey on the Reexamination of Faculty Roles and Rewards
The Carnegie Foundation for the Advancement of Teaching
5 Ivy Lane
Princeton, NJ 08540

APPENDIX B
RESULTS OF THE NATIONAL SURVEY ON
THE REEXAMINATION
OF FACULTY ROLES AND REWARDS, 1994

Table 1 IN THE PAST FIVE YEARS, HAS YOUR COLLEGE OR UNIVERSITY REEXAMINED FACULTY ROLES AND REWARDS?

Question 1	ALL INSTITUTIONS	RESEARCH	DOCTORATE-GRANTING	COMPRE-HENSIVE	LIBERAL ARTS
Yes, the review has been completed	21%	25%	15%	20%	22%
Yes, the review is still underway	45	48	55	47	39
No, but we plan to initiate a review soon	17	11	15	19	17
No, we do not plan to initiate a review soon	18	16	14	15	22

Source: The Carnegie Foundation for the Advancement of Teaching, National Survey on the Reexamination of Faculty Roles and Rewards, 1994.

Table 2 WHAT WERE THE MOST IMPORTANT REASONS FOR INITIATING THE EFFORT?
(Respondents could choose all that apply)

Question 2	ALL INSTITUTIONS	RESEARCH	DOCTORATE-GRANTING	COMPRE-HENSIVE	LIBERAL ARTS
Directive from the state legislature	4%	6%	16%	4%	0%
Directive from the system administration	7	7	14	9	3
Directive from the governing board	10	16	12	9	9
Leadership by this institution's president	50	58	57	50	47
Leadership by other administrators	68	70	63	68	67
Leadership by organized faculty	27	21	20	29	29
Concern of a few key faculty members	25	22	14	28	26
General dissatisfaction among faculty	14	15	12	13	15
Models from other colleges or universities	7	3	6	6	10
National reports on the state of higher education	20	31	24	24	12
Other	11	12	10	9	13

Source: The Carnegie Foundation for the Advancement of Teaching, National Survey on the Reexamination of Faculty Roles and Rewards, 1994.

Table 3 PLEASE INDICATE THE PRIMARY PROCEDURES YOU HAVE USED IN CONDUCTING THE REVIEW

(Respondents could choose all that apply)

Question 3	ALL INSTITUTIONS	RESEARCH	DOCTORATE-GRANTING	COMPRE-HENSIVE	LIBERAL ARTS
A trustee review committee was formed	3%	3%	2%	1%	5%
An all-campus review committee was formed	38	49	41	40	33
Each school executed an independent review	21	50	35	24	6
Each department executed an independent review	18	22	20	21	14
A chief academic officer led talks on faculty roles	52	53	41	48	57
A series of campus sessions were held to explore options	23	19	14	22	26
Other	23	9	25	21	28

Source: The Carnegie Foundation for the Advancement of Teaching, National Survey on the Reexamination of Faculty Roles and Rewards, 1994.

Table 4 HAVE ANY OF THE FOLLOWING ISSUES BEEN THE FOCUS OF YOUR REVIEW?

(Percentage responding "Yes")

Question 4	ALL INSTITUTIONS	RESEARCH	DOCTORATE-GRANTING	COMPRE-HENSIVE	LIBERAL ARTS
Clarifying institutional mission	69%	76%	67%	70%	65%
Redefining faculty roles	86	87	96	91	78
Striking a balance between institutional mission and faculty rewards	66	86	80	65	58
Improving the balance of time and effort faculty spend on various tasks	78	76	88	79	76

Source: The Carnegie Foundation for the Advancement of Teaching, National Survey on the Reexamination of Faculty Roles and Rewards, 1994.

Table 5 THE DEFINITION OF SCHOLARSHIP IS BEING BROADENED TO INCLUDE THE FULL RANGE OF ACTIVITIES IN WHICH FACULTY ARE ENGAGED

Question 5a	YES	NO
All Institutions	78%	22%
Research	66	34
Doctorate-Granting	79	21
Comprehensive	85	15
Liberal Arts	74	26

Source: The Carnegie Foundation for the Advancement of Teaching, National Survey on the Reexamination of Faculty Roles and Rewards, 1994.

Table 6 THE DEFINITION OF TEACHING IS BEING BROADENED TO INCLUDE ACTIVITIES SUCH AS CURRICULUM DEVELOPMENT, ADVISING, AND CONDUCTING INSTRUCTIONAL AND CLASSROOM RESEARCH

Question 5b	YES	NO
All Institutions	80%	20%
Research	80	20
Doctorate-Granting	89	11
Comprehensive	80	20
Liberal Arts	79	21

Source: The Carnegie Foundation for the Advancement of Teaching, National Survey on the Reexamination of Faculty Roles and Rewards, 1994.

Table 7 APPLIED SCHOLARSHIP (OUTREACH) IS BEING CLEARLY DISTINGUISHED FROM CAMPUS AND COMMUNITY CITIZENSHIP ACTIVITY

Question 5c	YES	NO
All Institutions	54%	46%
Research	48	52
Doctorate-Granting	55	45
Comprehensive	67	33
Liberal Arts	43	57

Source: The Carnegie Foundation for the Advancement of Teaching, National Survey on the Reexamination of Faculty Roles and Rewards, 1994.

Table 8 THE ROLE OF FACULTY AS CAMPUS CITIZENS (SERVICE TO THE INSTITUTION) IS BEING CLARIFIED

Question 5d	YES	NO
All Institutions	64%	36%
Research	47	53
Doctorate-Granting	54	46
Comprehensive	69	31
Liberal Arts	67	33

Source: The Carnegie Foundation for the Advancement of Teaching, National Survey on the Reexamination of Faculty Roles and Rewards, 1994.

Table 9 HAVE NEW METHODS OF EVALUATING FACULTY BEEN DEVELOPED IN THE FOLLOWING AREAS?
(Percentage responding "Yes")

Question 6	TEACHING	ADVISING	RESEARCH	CREATIVE WORK	APPLIED SCHOLARSHIP	SERVICE TO THE COLLEGE OR UNIVERSITY	SERVICE TO THE PROFESSION
All Institutions	69%	38%	34%	36%	38%	42%	33%
Research	77	28	16	24	39	22	19
Doctorate-Granting	66	39	33	31	47	33	30
Comprehensive	66	38	44	38	43	46	40
Liberal Arts	70	41	30	38	32	46	33

Source: The Carnegie Foundation for the Advancement of Teaching, National Survey on the Reexamination of Faculty Roles and Rewards, 1994.

Table 10 REGARDING RESEARCH, WHICH OF THE FOLLOWING METHODS OF EVALUATION ARE GENERALLY USED IN FACULTY EVALUATION AT YOUR INSTITUTION? . . . COUNTING NUMBERS OF PUBLICATIONS AND PRESENTATIONS, WEIGHTED BY TYPE

Question 7a	ALL INSTITUTIONS	RESEARCH	DOCTORATE-GRANTING	COMPRE-HENSIVE	LIBERAL ARTS
Yes, currently in general use	54%	87%	90%	58%	32%
No, not in general use but under consideration	8	1	2	7	13
No, not in general use and not under consideration at this time	37	12	8	35	53
Don't know	1	0	0	0	2

Source: The Carnegie Foundation for the Advancement of Teaching, National Survey on the Reexamination of Faculty Roles and Rewards, 1994.

Table 11 REGARDING RESEARCH, WHICH OF THE FOLLOWING METHODS OF EVALUATION ARE GENERALLY USED IN FACULTY EVALUATION AT YOUR INSTITUTION? . . . ASKING REVIEWERS TO USE SPECIFIC QUALITATIVE CRITERIA IN THEIR EVALUATIONS

Question 7b	ALL INSTITUTIONS	RESEARCH	DOCTORATE-GRANTING	COMPRE-HENSIVE	LIBERAL ARTS
Yes, currently in general use	44%	86%	66%	41%	27%
No, not in general use but under consideration	16	9	22	16	17
No, not in general use and not under consideration at this time	37	4	10	38	52
Don't know	4	1	2	4	4

Source: The Carnegie Foundation for the Advancement of Teaching, National Survey on the Reexamination of Faculty Roles and Rewards, 1994.

Table 12 REGARDING RESEARCH, WHICH OF THE FOLLOWING METHODS OF EVALUATION ARE GENERALLY USED IN FACULTY EVALUATION AT YOUR INSTITUTION? . . . SECURING JUDGMENTS BY OUTSIDE SCHOLARS

Question 7c	ALL INSTITUTIONS	RESEARCH	DOCTORATE-GRANTING	COMPRE-HENSIVE	LIBERAL ARTS
Yes, currently in general use	39%	100%	71%	25%	25%
No, not in general use but under consideration	17	0	10	20	19
No, not in general use and not under consideration at this time	43	0	18	53	52
Don't know	2	0	0	1	3

Source: The Carnegie Foundation for the Advancement of Teaching, National Survey on the Reexamination of Faculty Roles and Rewards, 1994.

Table 13 REGARDING RESEARCH, WHICH OF THE FOLLOWING METHODS OF EVALUATION ARE GENERALLY USED IN FACULTY EVALUATION AT YOUR INSTITUTION? . . . SECURING JUDGMENTS BY COLLEAGUES WITHIN THE INSTITUTION

Question 7d	ALL INSTITUTIONS	RESEARCH	DOCTORATE-GRANTING	COMPRE-HENSIVE	LIBERAL ARTS
Yes, currently in general use	73%	93%	83%	70%	67%
No, not in general use but under consideration	11	3	6	11	14
No, not in general use and not under consideration at this time	15	4	10	17	17
Don't know	1	0	0	1	1

Source: The Carnegie Foundation for the Advancement of Teaching, National Survey on the Reexamination of Faculty Roles and Rewards, 1994.

Table 14 REGARDING RESEARCH, WHICH OF THE FOLLOWING METHODS OF EVALUATION ARE GENERALLY USED IN FACULTY EVALUATION AT YOUR INSTITUTION? . . . SECURING SELF-EVALUATION OR PERSONAL STATEMENT

Question 7e	ALL INSTITUTIONS	RESEARCH	DOCTORATE-GRANTING	COMPRE-HENSIVE	LIBERAL ARTS
Yes, currently in general use	77%	69%	72%	75%	83%
No, not in general use but under consideration	9	13	6	11	7
No, not in general use and not under consideration at this time	11	13	20	12	8
Don't know	2	4	2	2	2

Source: The Carnegie Foundation for the Advancement of Teaching, National Survey on the Reexamination of Faculty Roles and Rewards, 1994.

Table 15 REGARDING RESEARCH, WHICH OF THE FOLLOWING METHODS OF EVALUATION ARE GENERALLY USED IN FACULTY EVALUATION AT YOUR INSTITUTION? . . . EVIDENCE OF STUDENT PARTICIPATION IN A RESEARCH PROJECT

Question 7f	ALL INSTITUTIONS	RESEARCH	DOCTORATE- GRANTING	COMPRE- HENSIVE	LIBERAL ARTS
Yes, currently in general use	37%	25%	32%	36%	43%
No, not in general use but under consideration	22	26	26	25	18
No, not in general use and not under consideration at this time	35	43	34	34	35
Don't know	5	6	8	5	4

Source: The Carnegie Foundation for the Advancement of Teaching, National Survey on the Reexamination of Faculty Roles and Rewards, 1994.

Table 16 REGARDING RESEARCH, WHICH OF THE FOLLOWING METHODS OF EVALUATION ARE GENERALLY USED IN FACULTY EVALUATION AT YOUR INSTITUTION? . . . EVIDENCE OF A RESEARCH PROJECT'S IMPACT ON TEACHING

Question 7g	ALL INSTITUTIONS	RESEARCH	DOCTORATE- GRANTING	COMPRE- HENSIVE	LIBERAL ARTS
Yes, currently in general use	42%	21%	24%	46%	50%
No, not in general use but under consideration	26	33	32	25	23
No, not in general use and not under consideration at this time	27	40	38	24	24
Don't know	5	6	6	5	3

Source: The Carnegie Foundation for the Advancement of Teaching, National Survey on the Reexamination of Faculty Roles and Rewards, 1994.

Table 17 REGARDING RESEARCH, WHICH OF THE FOLLOWING METHODS OF EVALUATION ARE GENERALLY USED IN FACULTY EVALUATION AT YOUR INSTITUTION? . . . EVIDENCE OF A RESEARCH PROJECT'S IMPACT ON APPLIED SCHOLARSHIP

Question 7h	ALL INSTITUTIONS	RESEARCH	DOCTORATE-GRANTING	COMPRE-HENSIVE	LIBERAL ARTS
Yes, currently in general use	34%	36%	34%	37%	31%
No, not in general use but under consideration	22	23	28	23	20
No, not in general use and not under consideration at this time	37	35	32	33	42
Don't know	7	6	6	7	7

Source: The Carnegie Foundation for the Advancement of Teaching, National Survey on the Reexamination of Faculty Roles and Rewards, 1994.

Table 18 REGARDING TEACHING, WHICH OF THE FOLLOWING METHODS OF EVALUATION ARE GENERALLY USED AT YOUR INSTITUTION FOR PURPOSES OF PROMOTION AND TENURE? . . . SELF-EVALUATION OR PERSONAL STATEMENT

Question 8a	ALL INSTITUTIONS	RESEARCH	DOCTORATE-GRANTING	COMPRE-HENSIVE	LIBERAL ARTS
Yes, currently in general use	82%	66%	74%	83%	88%
No, not in general use but under consideration	12	21	16	14	8
No, not in general use and not under consideration at this time	5	13	8	3	4
Don't know	0	0	2	0	0

Source: The Carnegie Foundation for the Advancement of Teaching, National Survey on the Reexamination of Faculty Roles and Rewards, 1994.

Table 19 REGARDING TEACHING, WHICH OF THE FOLLOWING METHODS OF EVALUATION ARE GENERALLY USED AT YOUR INSTITUTION FOR PURPOSES OF PROMOTION AND TENURE? . . . PEER REVIEW OF CLASSROOM TEACHING

Question 8b	ALL INSTITUTIONS	RESEARCH	DOCTORATE-GRANTING	COMPRE-HENSIVE	LIBERAL ARTS
Yes, currently in general use	58%	40%	41%	63%	62%
No, not in general use but under consideration	33	57	47	28	28
No, not in general use and not under consideration at this time	9	3	12	9	9
Don't know	0	0	0	0	0

Source: The Carnegie Foundation for the Advancement of Teaching, National Survey on the Reexamination of Faculty Roles and Rewards, 1994.

Table 20 REGARDING TEACHING, WHICH OF THE FOLLOWING METHODS OF EVALUATION ARE GENERALLY USED AT YOUR INSTITUTION FOR PURPOSES OF PROMOTION AND TENURE? . . . PEER REVIEW OF SYLLABI, EXAMINATIONS, AND OTHER TEACHING MATERIALS

Question 8c	ALL INSTITUTIONS	RESEARCH	DOCTORATE-GRANTING	COMPRE-HENSIVE	LIBERAL ARTS
Yes, currently in general use	62%	45%	56%	70%	61%
No, not in general use but under consideration	29	49	36	18	31
No, not in general use and not under consideration at this time	8	6	8	11	6
Don't know	1	0	0	1	1

Source: The Carnegie Foundation for the Advancement of Teaching, National Survey on the Reexamination of Faculty Roles and Rewards, 1994.

Table 21 REGARDING TEACHING, WHICH OF THE FOLLOWING METHODS OF EVALUATION ARE GENERALLY USED AT YOUR INSTITUTION FOR PURPOSES OF PROMOTION AND TENURE? . . . SYSTEMATIC STUDENT EVALUATIONS OF CLASSROOM TEACHING

Question 8d	ALL INSTITUTIONS	RESEARCH	DOCTORATE-GRANTING	COMPRE-HENSIVE	LIBERAL ARTS
Yes, currently in general use	98%	100%	96%	98%	98%
No, not in general use but under consideration	2	0	4	2	2
No, not in general use and not under consideration at this time	0	0	0	0	0
Don't know	0	0	0	0	0

Source: The Carnegie Foundation for the Advancement of Teaching, National Survey on the Reexamination of Faculty Roles and Rewards, 1994.

Table 22 REGARDING TEACHING, WHICH OF THE FOLLOWING METHODS OF EVALUATION ARE GENERALLY USED AT YOUR INSTITUTION FOR PURPOSES OF PROMOTION AND TENURE? . . . STUDENT EVALUATIONS OF ADVISING

Question 8e	ALL INSTITUTIONS	RESEARCH	DOCTORATE-GRANTING	COMPRE-HENSIVE	LIBERAL ARTS
Yes, currently in general use	24%	24%	14%	17%	33%
No, not in general use but under consideration	42	37	49	49	37
No, not in general use and not under consideration at this time	31	39	33	32	28
Don't know	2	0	4	2	2

Source: The Carnegie Foundation for the Advancement of Teaching, National Survey on the Reexamination of Faculty Roles and Rewards, 1994.

Table 23 REGARDING TEACHING, WHICH OF THE FOLLOWING METHODS OF EVALUATION ARE GENERALLY USED AT YOUR INSTITUTION FOR PURPOSES OF PROMOTION AND TENURE? . . . EVIDENCE OF STUDENT ACHIEVEMENT

Question 8f	ALL INSTITUTIONS	RESEARCH	DOCTORATE-GRANTING	COMPRE-HENSIVE	LIBERAL ARTS
Yes, currently in general use	24%	17%	18%	24%	28%
No, not in general use but under consideration	41	52	50	43	33
No, not in general use and not under consideration at this time	33	32	30	31	37
Don't know	2	0	2	2	2

Source: The Carnegie Foundation for the Advancement of Teaching, National Survey on the Reexamination of Faculty Roles and Rewards, 1994.

Table 24 REGARDING TEACHING, WHICH OF THE FOLLOWING METHODS OF EVALUATION ARE GENERALLY USED AT YOUR INSTITUTION FOR PURPOSES OF PROMOTION AND TENURE? . . . EVIDENCE OF CONTINUING STUDENT INTEREST

Question 8g	ALL INSTITUTIONS	RESEARCH	DOCTORATE-GRANTING	COMPRE-HENSIVE	LIBERAL ARTS
Yes, currently in general use	34%	24%	18%	33%	42%
No, not in general use but under consideration	26	33	29	26	24
No, not in general use and not under consideration at this time	37	40	49	38	33
Don't know	2	3	4	3	1

Source: The Carnegie Foundation for the Advancement of Teaching, National Survey on the Reexamination of Faculty Roles and Rewards, 1994.

Table 25 REGARDING TEACHING, WHICH OF THE FOLLOWING METHODS OF EVALUATION ARE GENERALLY USED AT YOUR INSTITUTION FOR PURPOSES OF PROMOTION AND TENURE?... ALUMNI OPINIONS

Question 8h	ALL INSTITUTIONS	RESEARCH	DOCTORATE-GRANTING	COMPRE-HENSIVE	LIBERAL ARTS
Yes, currently in general use	31%	24%	14%	30%	38%
No, not in general use but under consideration	29	36	41	31	24
No, not in general use and not under consideration at this time	38	39	43	38	37
Don't know	2	1	2	2	2

Source: The Carnegie Foundation for the Advancement of Teaching, National Survey on the Reexamination of Faculty Roles and Rewards, 1994.

Table 26 REGARDING TEACHING, WHICH OF THE FOLLOWING METHODS OF EVALUATION ARE GENERALLY USED AT YOUR INSTITUTION FOR PURPOSES OF PROMOTION AND TENURE?... EVIDENCE OF THE IMPACT OF TEACHING ON RESEARCH

Question 8i	ALL INSTITUTIONS	RESEARCH	DOCTORATE-GRANTING	COMPRE-HENSIVE	LIBERAL ARTS
Yes, currently in general use	15%	10%	14%	14%	17%
No, not in general use but under consideration	29	34	37	30	25
No, not in general use and not under consideration at this time	51	52	43	51	52
Don't know	5	3	6	4	6

Source: The Carnegie Foundation for the Advancement of Teaching, National Survey on the Reexamination of Faculty Roles and Rewards, 1994.

Table 27 REGARDING TEACHING, WHICH OF THE FOLLOWING METHODS OF EVALUATION ARE GENERALLY USED AT YOUR INSTITUTION FOR PURPOSES OF PROMOTION AND TENURE? . . . EVIDENCE OF THE IMPACT OF TEACHING ON APPLIED SCHOLARSHIP

Question 8j	ALL INSTITUTIONS	RESEARCH	DOCTORATE-GRANTING	COMPRE-HENSIVE	LIBERAL ARTS
Yes, currently in general use	14%	12%	16%	16%	13%
No, not in general use but under consideration	29	27	39	30	26
No, not in general use and not under consideration at this time	51	54	39	49	54
Don't know	6	7	6	5	7

Source: The Carnegie Foundation for the Advancement of Teaching, National Survey on the Reexamination of Faculty Roles and Rewards, 1994.

Table 28 REGARDING APPLIED SCHOLARSHIP, WHICH OF THE FOLLOWING METHODS OF EVALUATION ARE GENERALLY USED AT YOUR INSTITUTION FOR PURPOSES OF PROMOTION AND TENURE? . . . SELF-EVALUATION OR PERSONAL STATEMENT

Question 9a	ALL INSTITUTIONS	RESEARCH	DOCTORATE-GRANTING	COMPRE-HENSIVE	LIBERAL ARTS
Yes, currently in general use	74%	61%	72%	78%	76%
No, not in general use but under consideration	10	15	10	12	7
No, not in general use and not under consideration at this time	13	23	12	9	13
Don't know	3	2	6	1	3

Source: The Carnegie Foundation for the Advancement of Teaching, National Survey on the Reexamination of Faculty Roles and Rewards, 1994.

Table 29 REGARDING APPLIED SCHOLARSHIP, WHICH OF THE FOLLOWING METHODS OF EVALUATION ARE GENERALLY USED AT YOUR INSTITUTION FOR PURPOSES OF PROMOTION AND TENURE? . . . CLIENT OR USER EVALUATION

Question 9b	ALL INSTITUTIONS	RESEARCH	DOCTORATE-GRANTING	COMPRE-HENSIVE	LIBERAL ARTS
Yes, currently in general use	35%	49%	41%	40%	26%
No, not in general use but under consideration	23	19	22	25	22
No, not in general use and not under consideration at this time	38	27	29	33	48
Don't know	4	4	8	2	5

Source: The Carnegie Foundation for the Advancement of Teaching, National Survey on the Reexamination of Faculty Roles and Rewards, 1994.

Table 30 REGARDING APPLIED SCHOLARSHIP, WHICH OF THE FOLLOWING METHODS OF EVALUATION ARE GENERALLY USED AT YOUR INSTITUTION FOR PURPOSES OF PROMOTION AND TENURE? . . . EVALUATIONS OF THE PROJECT BY SPECIALISTS

Question 9c	ALL INSTITUTIONS	RESEARCH	DOCTORATE-GRANTING	COMPRE-HENSIVE	LIBERAL ARTS
Yes, currently in general use	23%	50%	26%	25%	11%
No, not in general use but under consideration	22	15	32	24	21
No, not in general use and not under consideration at this time	50	27	38	48	61
Don't know	5	8	4	3	7

Source: The Carnegie Foundation for the Advancement of Teaching, National Survey on the Reexamination of Faculty Roles and Rewards, 1994.

Table 31 REGARDING APPLIED SCHOLARSHIP, WHICH OF THE FOLLOWING METHODS OF EVALUATION ARE GENERALLY USED AT YOUR INSTITUTION FOR PURPOSES OF PROMOTION AND TENURE?... EVIDENCE OF STUDENT PARTICIPATION IN A PROJECT

Question 9d	ALL INSTITUTIONS	RESEARCH	DOCTORATE-GRANTING	COMPRE-HENSIVE	LIBERAL ARTS
Yes, currently in general use	32%	16%	28%	33%	37%
No, not in general use but under consideration	26	27	24	30	21
No, not in general use and not under consideration at this time	37	48	40	32	37
Don't know	6	9	8	5	5

Source: The Carnegie Foundation for the Advancement of Teaching, National Survey on the Reexamination of Faculty Roles and Rewards, 1994.

Table 32 REGARDING APPLIED SCHOLARSHIP, WHICH OF THE FOLLOWING METHODS OF EVALUATION ARE GENERALLY USED AT YOUR INSTITUTION FOR PURPOSES OF PROMOTION AND TENURE?... EVIDENCE OF THE IMPACT OF APPLIED SCHOLARSHIP ON TEACHING

Question 9e	ALL INSTITUTIONS	RESEARCH	DOCTORATE-GRANTING	COMPRE-HENSIVE	LIBERAL ARTS
Yes, currently in general use	30%	21%	26%	32%	31%
No, not in general use but under consideration	26	24	34	28	23
No, not in general use and not under consideration at this time	38	43	36	33	41
Don't know	7	12	4	7	5

Source: The Carnegie Foundation for the Advancement of Teaching, National Survey on the Reexamination of Faculty Roles and Rewards, 1994.

Table 33 REGARDING APPLIED SCHOLARSHIP, WHICH OF THE FOLLOWING METHODS OF EVALUATION ARE GENERALLY USED AT YOUR INSTITUTION FOR PURPOSES OF PROMOTION AND TENURE: . . . EVIDENCE OF THE IMPACT OF APPLIED SCHOLARSHIP ON FUTURE RESEARCH

Question 9f	ALL INSTITUTIONS	RESEARCH	DOCTORATE-GRANTING	COMPRE-HENSIVE	LIBERAL ARTS
Yes, currently in general use	20%	27%	36%	21%	13%
No, not in general use but under consideration	24	25	22	24	23
No, not in general use and not under consideration at this time	48	37	36	47	56
Don't know	8	10	6	9	8

Source: The Carnegie Foundation for the Advancement of Teaching, National Survey on the Reexamination of Faculty Roles and Rewards, 1994.

Table 34 THINKING ABOUT YOUR OWN SITUATION, DO THE FOLLOWING FACULTY ACTIVITIES COUNT MORE OR LESS TODAY—FOR PURPOSES OF FACULTY ADVANCEMENT—THAN THEY DID FIVE YEARS AGO? . . . RESEARCH

Question 10a	ALL INSTITUTIONS	RESEARCH	DOCTORATE-GRANTING	COMPRE-HENSIVE	LIBERAL ARTS
Count more today than five years ago	41%	22%	41%	48%	41%
Count less today than five years ago	10	9	18	11	8
Count about the same as five years ago	48	70	41	41	51
Don't know	0	0	0	1	0

Source: The Carnegie Foundation for the Advancement of Teaching, National Survey on the Reexamination of Faculty Roles and Rewards, 1994.

Table 35 THINKING ABOUT YOUR OWN SITUATION, DO THE FOLLOWING FACULTY ACTIVITIES COUNT MORE OR LESS TODAY—FOR PURPOSES OF FACULTY ADVANCEMENT—THAN THEY DID FIVE YEARS AGO? . . . TEACHING

Question 10b	ALL INSTITUTIONS	RESEARCH	DOCTORATE-GRANTING	COMPRE-HENSIVE	LIBERAL ARTS
Count more today than five years ago	59%	81%	67%	58%	52%
Count less today than five years ago	3	4	4	4	1
Count about the same as five years ago	38	14	29	36	47
Don't know	0	0	0	1	0

Source: The Carnegie Foundation for the Advancement of Teaching, National Survey on the Reexamination of Faculty Roles and Rewards, 1994.

Table 36 THINKING ABOUT YOUR OWN SITUATION, DO THE FOLLOWING FACULTY ACTIVITIES COUNT MORE OR LESS TODAY—FOR PURPOSES OF FACULTY ADVANCEMENT—THAN THEY DID FIVE YEARS AGO? . . . APPLIED SCHOLARSHIP (OUTREACH)

Question 10c	ALL INSTITUTIONS	RESEARCH	DOCTORATE-GRANTING	COMPRE-HENSIVE	LIBERAL ARTS
Count more today than five years ago	42%	38%	49%	49%	33%
Count less today than five years ago	6	1	12	5	8
Count about the same as five years ago	46	59	33	42	48
Don't know	6	1	6	3	11

Source: The Carnegie Foundation for the Advancement of Teaching, National Survey on the Reexamination of Faculty Roles and Rewards, 1994.

Table 37 THINKING ABOUT YOUR OWN SITUATION, DO THE FOLLOWING FACULTY ACTIVITIES COUNT MORE OR LESS TODAY—FOR PURPOSES OF FACULTY ADVANCEMENT—THAN THEY DID FIVE YEARS AGO? . . . SERVICE TO THE INSTITUTION (CITIZENSHIP)

Question 10d	ALL INSTITUTIONS	RESEARCH	DOCTORATE-GRANTING	COMPRE-HENSIVE	LIBERAL ARTS
Count more today than five years ago	26%	6%	14%	29%	32%
Count less today than five years ago	13	9	22	15	10
Count about the same as five years ago	60	86	65	56	56
Don't know	1	0	0	1	2

Source: The Carnegie Foundation for the Advancement of Teaching, National Survey on the Reexamination of Faculty Roles and Rewards, 1994.

Table 38 THINKING ABOUT YOUR OWN SITUATION, DO THE FOLLOWING FACULTY ACTIVITIES COUNT MORE OR LESS TODAY—FOR PURPOSES OF FACULTY ADVANCEMENT—THAN THEY DID FIVE YEARS AGO? . . . PROFESSIONAL ACTIVITY (NATIONAL COMMITTEES, ETC.)

Question 10e	ALL INSTITUTIONS	RESEARCH	DOCTORATE-GRANTING	COMPRE-HENSIVE	LIBERAL ARTS
Count more today than five years ago	25%	6%	12%	31%	29%
Count less today than five years ago	8	10	6	7	8
Count about the same as five years ago	66	84	82	61	61
Don't know	1	0	0	2	2

Source: The Carnegie Foundation for the Advancement of Teaching, National Survey on the Reexamination of Faculty Roles and Rewards, 1994.

Table 39 MANY INSTITUTIONS HAVE DEVELOPED NEW WAYS TO REWARD GOOD TEACHING. WHICH OF THE FOLLOWING PRACTICES ARE NOW IN PLACE OR ARE BEING CONSIDERED AT YOUR INSTITUTION? . . . MERIT INCREASES FOR TEACHING EXCELLENCE

Question 11a	NOW IN PLACE	UNDER CONSIDERATION	NOT UNDER CONSIDERATION	DON'T KNOW
All Institutions	50%	25%	25%	0%
Research	68	28	4	0
Doctorate-Granting	71	16	14	0
Comprehensive	43	26	30	0
Liberal Arts	47	24	28	0

Source: The Carnegie Foundation for the Advancement of Teaching, National Survey on the Reexamination of Faculty Roles and Rewards, 1994.

Table 40 MANY INSTITUTIONS HAVE DEVELOPED NEW WAYS TO REWARD GOOD TEACHING. WHICH OF THE FOLLOWING PRACTICES ARE NOW IN PLACE OR ARE BEING CONSIDERED AT YOUR INSTITUTION? . . . SPECIAL AWARDS FOR TEACHING EXCELLENCE

Question 11b	NOW IN PLACE	UNDER CONSIDERATION	NOT UNDER CONSIDERATION	DON'T KNOW
All Institutions	78%	12%	10%	0%
Research	99	1	0	0
Doctorate-Granting	88	8	4	0
Comprehensive	77	13	10	0
Liberal Arts	70	15	15	0

Source: The Carnegie Foundation for the Advancement of Teaching, National Survey on the Reexamination of Faculty Roles and Rewards, 1994.

Table 41 MANY INSTITUTIONS HAVE DEVELOPED NEW WAYS TO REWARD GOOD TEACHING. WHICH OF THE FOLLOWING PRACTICES ARE NOW IN PLACE OR ARE BEING CONSIDERED AT YOUR INSTITUTION? . . . DISTINGUISHED CHAIRS FOR TEACHING EXCELLENCE

Question 11c	NOW IN PLACE	UNDER CONSIDERATION	NOT UNDER CONSIDERATION	DON'T KNOW
All Institutions	23%	23%	53%	1%
Research	35	33	30	1
Doctorate-Granting	22	28	46	4
Comprehensive	19	20	60	1
Liberal Arts	23	20	56	1

Source: The Carnegie Foundation for the Advancement of Teaching, National Survey on the Reexamination of Faculty Roles and Rewards, 1994.

Table 42 MANY INSTITUTIONS HAVE DEVELOPED NEW WAYS TO REWARD GOOD TEACHING. WHICH OF THE FOLLOWING PRACTICES ARE NOW IN PLACE OR ARE BEING CONSIDERED AT YOUR INSTITUTION? . . . USING DISTINGUISHED TEACHERS AS MENTORS

Question 11d	NOW IN PLACE	UNDER CONSIDERATION	NOT UNDER CONSIDERATION	DON'T KNOW
All Institutions	37%	39%	22%	1%
Research	41	45	13	1
Doctorate-Granting	39	45	12	4
Comprehensive	37	40	23	0
Liberal Arts	37	36	26	1

Source: The Carnegie Foundation for the Advancement of Teaching, National Survey on the Reexamination of Faculty Roles and Rewards, 1994.

Table 43 MANY INSTITUTIONS HAVE DEVELOPED NEW WAYS TO REWARD GOOD TEACHING. WHICH OF THE FOLLOWING PRACTICES ARE NOW IN PLACE OR ARE BEING CONSIDERED AT YOUR INSTITUTION? . . . GRANTS FOR COURSE DEVELOPMENT

Question 11e	NOW IN PLACE	UNDER CONSIDERATION	NOT UNDER CONSIDERATION	DON'T KNOW
All Institutions	68%	16%	15%	1%
Research	83	10	6	1
Doctorate-Granting	73	22	4	2
Comprehensive	71	13	14	1
Liberal Arts	59	19	21	0

Source: The Carnegie Foundation for the Advancement of Teaching, National Survey on the Reexamination of Faculty Roles and Rewards, 1994.

Table 44 MANY INSTITUTIONS HAVE DEVELOPED NEW WAYS TO REWARD GOOD TEACHING. WHICH OF THE FOLLOWING PRACTICES ARE NOW IN PLACE OR ARE BEING CONSIDERED AT YOUR INSTITUTION? . . . RELEASE TIME FOR COURSE DEVELOPMENT

Question 11f	NOW IN PLACE	UNDER CONSIDERATION	NOT UNDER CONSIDERATION	DON'T KNOW
All Institutions	58%	18%	24%	1%
Research	75	10	14	0
Doctorate-Granting	73	16	8	4
Comprehensive	62	15	22	1
Liberal Arts	45	23	31	0

Source: The Carnegie Foundation for the Advancement of Teaching, National Survey on the Reexamination of Faculty Roles and Rewards, 1994.

Table 45 MANY INSTITUTIONS HAVE DEVELOPED NEW WAYS TO REWARD GOOD TEACHING. WHICH OF THE FOLLOWING PRACTICES ARE NOW IN PLACE OR ARE BEING CONSIDERED AT YOUR INSTITUTION? . . . TRAVEL FUNDS FOR TEACHING IMPROVEMENT PURPOSES

Question 11g	NOW IN PLACE	UNDER CONSIDERATION	NOT UNDER CONSIDERATION	DON'T KNOW
All Institutions	79%	11%	10%	1%
Research	66	19	15	0
Doctorate-Granting	69	16	16	0
Comprehensive	82	8	9	1
Liberal Arts	82	10	7	0

Source: The Carnegie Foundation for the Advancement of Teaching, National Survey on the Reexamination of Faculty Roles and Rewards, 1994.

Table 46 MANY INSTITUTIONS HAVE DEVELOPED NEW WAYS TO REWARD GOOD TEACHING. WHICH OF THE FOLLOWING PRACTICES ARE NOW IN PLACE OR ARE BEING CONSIDERED AT YOUR INSTITUTION? . . . SABBATICALS FOR TEACHING IMPROVEMENT PURPOSES

Question 11h	NOW IN PLACE	UNDER CONSIDERATION	NOT UNDER CONSIDERATION	DON'T KNOW
All Institutions	74%	12%	14%	0%
Research	65	9	25	1
Doctorate-Granting	64	18	18	0
Comprehensive	73	13	14	0
Liberal Arts	80	10	10	0

Source: The Carnegie Foundation for the Advancement of Teaching, National Survey on the Reexamination of Faculty Roles and Rewards, 1994.

Table 47 MANY INSTITUTIONS HAVE DEVELOPED NEW WAYS TO REWARD GOOD TEACHING. WHICH OF THE FOLLOWING PRACTICES ARE NOW IN PLACE OR ARE BEING CONSIDERED AT YOUR INSTITUTION? . . . A CENTER FOR TEACHING IMPROVEMENT

Question 11i	NOW IN PLACE	UNDER CONSIDERATION	NOT UNDER CONSIDERATION	DON'T KNOW
All Institutions	28%	33%	37%	1%
Research	61	29	10	0
Doctorate-Granting	41	37	22	0
Comprehensive	29	42	29	1
Liberal Arts	15	26	58	1

Source: The Carnegie Foundation for the Advancement of Teaching, National Survey on the Reexamination of Faculty Roles and Rewards, 1994.

Table 48 MANY TENURE ISSUES ARE NOW SURFACING AT COLLEGES AND UNIVERSITIES. HAVE ANY OF THE FOLLOWING PRACTICES BEEN IMPLEMENTED AT YOUR INSTITUTION IN THE PAST FIVE YEARS? . . . CHANGES IN THE CRITERIA BY WHICH TENURE IS AWARDED

Question 12a	ALL INSTITUTIONS	RESEARCH	DOCTORATE-GRANTING	COMPRE-HENSIVE	LIBERAL ARTS
Yes	39%	23%	38%	46%	37%
No, but under consideration	22	30	28	21	19
No, not under consideration at this time	34	45	34	29	35
Don't know/Not applicable	5	1	0	4	10

Source: The Carnegie Foundation for the Advancement of Teaching, National Survey on the Reexamination of Faculty Roles and Rewards, 1994.

Table 49 MANY TENURE ISSUES ARE NOW SURFACING AT COLLEGES AND UNIVERSITIES. HAVE ANY OF THE FOLLOWING PRACTICES BEEN IMPLEMENTED AT YOUR INSTITUTION IN THE PAST FIVE YEARS? . . . REGULAR POST-TENURE REVIEW OF FACULTY

Question 12b	ALL INSTITUTIONS	RESEARCH	DOCTORATE-GRANTING	COMPRE-HENSIVE	LIBERAL ARTS
Yes	46%	41%	43%	44%	51%
No, but under consideration	28	38	35	29	23
No, not under consideration at this time	19	20	20	21	15
Don't know/Not applicable	7	1	2	6	11

Source: The Carnegie Foundation for the Advancement of Teaching, National Survey on the Reexamination of Faculty Roles and Rewards, 1994.

Table 50 MANY TENURE ISSUES ARE NOW SURFACING AT COLLEGES AND UNIVERSITIES. HAVE ANY OF THE FOLLOWING PRACTICES BEEN IMPLEMENTED AT YOUR INSTITUTION IN THE PAST FIVE YEARS? . . . NEGOTIATING THE LENGTH OF THE PROBATION PERIOD PRIOR TO TENURE WITH INDIVIDUAL FACULTY

Question 12c	ALL INSTITUTIONS	RESEARCH	DOCTORATE-GRANTING	COMPRE-HENSIVE	LIBERAL ARTS
Yes	26%	17%	31%	27%	27%
No, but under consideration	9	13	2	9	9
No, not under consideration at this time	58	67	63	58	53
Don't know/Not applicable	7	3	4	6	11

Source: The Carnegie Foundation for the Advancement of Teaching, National Survey on the Reexamination of Faculty Roles and Rewards, 1994.

Table 51 MANY TENURE ISSUES ARE NOW SURFACING AT COLLEGES AND UNIVERSITIES. HAVE ANY OF THE FOLLOWING PRACTICES BEEN IMPLEMENTED AT YOUR INSTITUTION IN THE PAST FIVE YEARS? . . . ALTERNATIVE CONTRACTUAL ARRANGEMENTS THAT DO NOT INCLUDE TENURE

Question 12d	ALL INSTITUTIONS	RESEARCH	DOCTORATE-GRANTING	COMPRE-HENSIVE	LIBERAL ARTS
Yes	34%	32%	38%	34%	34%
No, but under consideration	17	13	18	18	17
No, not under consideration at this time	44	53	42	44	42
Don't know/Not applicable	4	1	2	3	7

Source: The Carnegie Foundation for the Advancement of Teaching, National Survey on the Reexamination of Faculty Roles and Rewards, 1994.

Table 52 MANY TENURE ISSUES ARE NOW SURFACING AT COLLEGES AND UNIVERSITIES. HAVE ANY OF THE FOLLOWING PRACTICES BEEN IMPLEMENTED AT YOUR INSTITUTION IN THE PAST FIVE YEARS? . . . ABOLISHING TENURE

Question 12e	ALL INSTITUTIONS	RESEARCH	DOCTORATE-GRANTING	COMPRE-HENSIVE	LIBERAL ARTS
Yes	3%	0%	0%	4%	4%
No, but under consideration	4	0	4	4	5
No, not under consideration at this time	88	100	94	89	81
Don't know/Not applicable	5	0	2	3	11

Source: The Carnegie Foundation for the Advancement of Teaching, National Survey on the Reexamination of Faculty Roles and Rewards, 1994.

Table 53 HAVE THE FOLLOWING IDEAS ABOUT FACULTY ROLES AND REWARDS BEEN INTRODUCED OR CONSIDERED AT YOUR INSTITUTION?: . . . ENCOURAGING FACULTY TO SHIFT THEIR SCHOLARLY FOCUS FROM TIME TO TIME (CONCENTRATING ON TEACHING, THEN RESEARCH, FOR EXAMPLE)

Question 13a	ALL INSTITUTIONS	RESEARCH	DOCTORATE-GRANTING	COMPRE-HENSIVE	LIBERAL ARTS
Yes	29%	33%	36%	37%	18%
No, but under consideration	23	35	24	21	21
No, not under consideration at this time	44	30	36	38	56
Don't know/Not applicable	4	1	4	4	4

Source: The Carnegie Foundation for the Advancement of Teaching, National Survey on the Reexamination of Faculty Roles and Rewards, 1994.

Table 54 HAVE THE FOLLOWING IDEAS ABOUT FACULTY ROLES AND REWARDS BEEN INTRODUCED OR CONSIDERED AT YOUR INSTITUTION?: . . . EVALUATING DEPARTMENTAL PERFORMANCE, NOT JUST INDIVIDUALS

Question 13b	ALL INSTITUTIONS	RESEARCH	DOCTORATE-GRANTING	COMPRE-HENSIVE	LIBERAL ARTS
Yes	31%	37%	43%	26%	32%
No, but under consideration	30	49	22	33	24
No, not under consideration at this time	37	15	35	40	41
Don't know/Not applicable	1	0	0	1	3

Source: The Carnegie Foundation for the Advancement of Teaching, National Survey on the Reexamination of Faculty Roles and Rewards, 1994.

Table 55 HAVE THE FOLLOWING IDEAS ABOUT FACULTY ROLES AND REWARDS BEEN INTRODUCED OR CONSIDERED AT YOUR INSTITUTION? . . . WORKING COLLABORATIVELY WITH OTHER INSTITUTIONS IN DEVELOPING NEW APPROACHES IN FACULTY ROLES AND REWARDS

Question 13c	ALL INSTITUTIONS	RESEARCH	DOCTORATE-GRANTING	COMPRE-HENSIVE	LIBERAL ARTS
Yes	20%	19%	20%	22%	18%
No, but under consideration	25	19	25	28	25
No, not under consideration at this time	52	61	53	47	53
Don't know/Not applicable	3	0	2	3	4

Source: The Carnegie Foundation for the Advancement of Teaching, National Survey on the Reexamination of Faculty Roles and Rewards, 1994.

Table 56 HAS *SCHOLARSHIP RECONSIDERED*, THE 1990 CARNEGIE FOUNDATION REPORT, PLAYED A ROLE IN THE DISCUSSION ABOUT FACULTY ROLES AND REWARDS AT YOUR INSTITUTION?

Question 14	YES	NO
All Institutions	62%	38%
Research	65	35
Doctorate-Granting	74	26
Comprehensive	72	28
Liberal Arts	50	50

Source: The Carnegie Foundation for the Advancement of Teaching, National Survey on the Reexamination of Faculty Roles and Rewards, 1994.

Table 57 IN THE PAST FIVE YEARS, HAS YOUR INSTITUTION DEVELOPED NEW APPROACHES TO ANY OF THE FOLLOWING?

(Percentage responding "Yes")

Question 15	ALL INSTITUTIONS	RESEARCH	DOCTORATE-GRANTING	COMPRE-HENSIVE	LIBERAL ARTS
General education for undergraduates	77%	77%	83%	76%	76%
Quality of campus life	85	90	90	83	84
Public and community service for students	73	68	81	72	75
Technology for teaching and learning	94	97	96	96	92
Assessment of student learning	82	60	76	89	82

Source: The Carnegie Foundation for the Advancement of Teaching, National Survey on the Reexamination of Faculty Roles and Rewards, 1994.

APPENDIX C
TECHNICAL NOTES

I N RESPONSE TO A GROWING INTEREST in broadening the definition of scholarship, The Carnegie Foundation for the Advancement of Teaching initiated a study to examine changes in policies and procedures with regard to faculty evaluation. A questionnaire administered to chief academic officers contributed significantly to this study by helping map the scope, direction, and progress of efforts on the nation's campuses to reexamine faculty roles and rewards.

The National Survey on the Reexamination of Faculty Roles and Rewards was developed by the staff of The Carnegie Foundation in consultation with several experts on the evaluation of faculty. Questionnaires were mailed in the fall of 1994 to chief academic officers at all four-year institutions classified as Research Universities, Doctorate-Granting Universities, Comprehensive Universities and Colleges, and Liberal Arts Colleges in the 1987 *Classification of Institutions of Higher Education.*

A total of 1,380 survey instruments was mailed; completed questionnaires were received from 865 chief academic officers. The overall response rate was 63 percent, ranging from 54 percent for Doctorate-Granting Universities II to 78 percent for Doctorate-Granting Universities I.

In analyzing the data collected in this survey, it is important to note that the first question screens out respondents who have not reexamined faculty roles and rewards. This means that of the 865 respondents, 296 did not complete the full set of questions on the survey instrument because they had not been involved in such a review process. All respondents were asked to complete the first question and question 15. Questions 2 through 14 were completed only by respondents who were reporting from colleges or universities that have reexamined faculty roles and rewards in the past five years.

The questionnaire used in the National Survey on the Reexamination of Faculty Roles and Rewards is included in Appendix A. Appendix B presents tables for each of the quantifiable questions. The results to each question are disaggregated by Carnegie Classification category. The Carnegie Classification is discussed in Appendix D.

APPENDIX D
CARNEGIE CLASSIFICATIONS

A T THE TIME the background research and survey work were being conducted for this report, the 1987 edition of The Carnegie Foundation's *A Classification of Institutions of Higher Education* was the most recent version available. Thus, the National Survey on the Reexamination of Faculty Roles and Rewards employed the 1987 *Classification* in the sampling methodology.

A Classification of Institutions of Higher Education, 1987 Edition includes all colleges and universities in the United States listed in the 1985–86 *Higher Education General Information Survey of Institutional Characteristics*. It groups 3,389 institutions into ten categories on the basis of the level of degree offered, ranging from prebaccalaureate to the doctorate, and the comprehensiveness of their missions. The categories are as follows:

1. *Research Universities I*. These institutions offer a full range of baccalaureate programs, are committed to graduate education through the doctorate degree, and give high priority to research. They receive annually at least $33.5 million in federal support and award at least fifty Ph.D. degrees each year.

2. *Research Universities II*. These institutions offer a full range of baccalaureate programs, are committed to graduate education through the doctorate degree, and give high priority to research. They receive annually at least $12.5 million in federal support and award at least fifty Ph.D. degrees each year.

3. *Doctorate-Granting Universities I.* In addition to offering a full range of baccalaureate programs, the mission of these institutions includes a commitment to graduate education through the doctorate degree. They award at least forty Ph.D. degrees annually in five or more academic disciplines.

4. *Doctorate-Granting Universities II.* In addition to offering a full range of baccalaureate programs, the mission of these institutions includes a commitment to graduate education through the doctorate degree. They award annually twenty or more Ph.D. degrees in at least one discipline or ten or more Ph.D. degrees in three or more disciplines.

5. *Comprehensive Universities and Colleges I.* These institutions offer baccalaureate programs and, with few exceptions, graduate education through the master's degree. More than half of their baccalaureate degrees are awarded in two or more occupational or professional disciplines such as engineering or business administration. All of the institutions in this group enroll at least twenty-five hundred students.

6. *Comprehensive Universities and Colleges II.* These institutions award more than half of their baccalaureate degrees in two or more occupational or professional disciplines, such as engineering or business administration, and many also offer graduate education through the master's degree. All of the institutions in this group enroll between fifteen hundred and twenty-five hundred students.

7. *Liberal Arts Colleges I.* These highly selective institutions are primarily undergraduate colleges that award more than half of their baccalaureate degrees in arts and science fields.

8. *Liberal Arts Colleges II.* These institutions are primarily undergraduate colleges that are less selective and award more than half of their degrees in liberal arts fields. This category also includes a group of colleges that award less than half of their degrees in liberal arts fields but, with fewer than fifteen hundred students, are too small to be considered comprehensive.

9. *Two-Year Community, Junior, and Technical Colleges.* These institutions offer certificate or degree programs through the associate of arts level and, with few exceptions, offer no baccalaureate degrees.

10. *Professional Schools and Other Specialized Institutions.* These institutions offer degrees ranging from the bachelor's to the doctorate. At least 50 percent of the degrees awarded by these institutions are in a single specialized field. Specialized institutions include:

Theological seminaries, Bible colleges, and other institutions offering degrees in religion

Medical schools and medical centers

Other separate health profession schools

Schools of law

Schools of engineering and technology

Schools of business and management

Schools of art, music, and design

Teachers colleges

Other specialized institutions

Corporate-sponsored institutions

In 1994, a new edition of *A Classification of Institutions of Higher Education* was released by The Carnegie Foundation for the Advancement of Teaching. While every effort was made to maintain the general framework of the classification over time, the definitions in the 1994 edition were modified somewhat to clarify the groupings.

The most consequential change to the definitions in the 1994 edition is an increased emphasis on the highest level of degree conferred. The names of the classification categories have been changed to reflect this shift in emphasis. Thus, the "Two-Year Community, Junior, and Technical Colleges" are now called "Associate of Arts Colleges"; the "Liberal Arts Colleges" are now referred to as "Baccalaureate Colleges"; and "Comprehensive Universities and Colleges" are now called "Master's Colleges and Universities." The "Doctorate-Granting Universities" labels have been changed to "Doctoral Universities"; the "Research Universities" titles remain the same.

NOTES

Preface

1. Burton R. Clark, *The Academic Life: Small Worlds, Different Worlds* (Princeton, N.J.: Carnegie Foundation for the Advancement of Teaching, 1987), pp. 98–99.

2. Ernest L. Boyer, *College: The Undergraduate Experience in America* (New York: Harper-Collins, 1987), pp. 290–291.

3. Carnegie Foundation for the Advancement of Teaching, *Campus Life: In Search of Community* (Princeton, N.J.: author, 1990), p. 9.

Chapter One

1. Robert K. Merton, "*Recognition* and *Excellence*: Instructive Ambiguities," in *The Sociology of Science: Theoretical and Empirical Investigations,* ed. Norman W. Storer (Chicago: University of Chicago Press, 1973), pp. 419–438.

2. Charles William Eliot, *Educational Reform* (1898; reprint, New York: Arno Press and *New York Times,* 1969), p. 27.

3. Frederick Rudolph, *The American College and University: A History* (New York: Knopf, 1962), p. 229.

4. Laurence R. Veysey, *The Emergence of the American University* (Chicago: University of Chicago Press, 1965), p. 61.

5. Rudolph (1962), p. 352.

6. Clara M. Lovett, "To Affect Intimately the Lives of the People: American Professors and Their Society," *Change* (July/Aug. 1993), p. 36.

7. James S. Fairweather, *Teaching, Research, and Faculty Rewards: A Summary of the Research Findings of the Faculty Profile Project* (University Park, Pa.: National Center on Postsecondary Teaching, Learning and Assessment, Pennsylvania State University, 1993), p. 1.

8. Fairweather (1993), p. 11.

9. David Riesman, *Constraint and Variety in American Education* (Garden City, N.Y.: Anchor Books, 1958), p. 35.

10. Woodrow Wilson, "Princeton in the Nation's Service," in *American Higher Education: A Documentary History,* vol. II, ed. Richard Hofstadter and Wilson Smith (Chicago: University of Chicago Press, 1961), pp. 684–695.

11. J. Robert Oppenheimer, "Prospects in the Arts and Sciences," *New York Times,* Dec. 12, 1954, sec. D, p. 27.

12. Russell Edgerton, "Evaluating Teaching as Scholarly Work," keynote address, 1995 Academic Affairs Symposium, University of Georgia, Athens, Ga., Apr. 7–8, 1995.

13. American Association of University Professors, "The Work of Faculty: Expectations, Priorities, and Rewards," *Academe* (Jan.–Feb. 1994), p. 35.

14. Robert M. Diamond and Bronwyn E. Adam, eds., *The Disciplines Speak: Rewarding the Scholarly, Professional, and Creative Work of Faculty* (Washington, D.C.: American Association for Higher Education, 1995).

15. Joint Policy Board for Mathematics, "Recognition and Rewards in the Mathematical Sciences," in Diamond and Adam (1995), pp. 65–66.

16. American Historical Association, "Redefining Historical Scholarship," in Diamond and Adam (1995), pp. 29–31.

17. American Association for Higher Education, "The Engaged Campus," National Conference on Higher Education, Washington, D.C., Mar. 1995.

18. American Association of University Professors, "Professors as Citizens," annual meeting, Washington, D.C., June 7–11, 1995.

19. R. Eugene Rice, welcoming remarks in printed program, Third AAHE Conference on Faculty Roles and Rewards, "From 'My Work' to 'Our Work': Realigning Faculty Work with College and University Purposes," Phoenix, Ariz., Jan. 19–22, 1995, p. 1.

20. Joint Policy Board for Mathematics (1995), p. 66.

21. Association of American Geographers, "Statement," in Diamond and Adam (1995), pp. 43–44.

22. American Chemical Society, "Report of the Task Force on the Definition of Scholarship in Chemistry, 1993"; reprinted in Bronwyn Adam and Alton Roberts, "Differences Among the Disciplines," in *Recognizing Faculty Work: Reward Systems for the Year 2000,* ed. Robert Diamond and Bronwyn Adam (San Francisco: Jossey-Bass, 1993), p. 47.

23. Robert A. McCaughey, *Scholars and Teachers: The Faculties of Select Liberal Arts Colleges and Their Place in American Higher Learning* (New York: Conceptual Litho Reproductions, 1994), p. 25.

24. Peter Seldin, *Changing Practices in Faculty Evaluation* (San Francisco: Jossey-Bass, 1984), p. 42.

25. Seldin (1984), p. 74.

26. Peter Seldin, "How Colleges Evaluate Professors 1983 v. 1993," *AAHE Bulletin* (Oct. 1993) pp. 6–12.

27. Neal Whitman and Elaine Weiss, Overview to *Faculty Evaluation: The Use of Explicit Criteria for Promotion, Retention, and Tenure* (Washington, D.C.: American Association for Higher Education, 1982), p. 1.

28. Ernest L. Boyer, Philip G. Altbach, and Mary Jean Whitelaw, *The Academic Profession: An International Perspective* (Princeton, N.J.: The Carnegie Foundation for the Advancement of Teaching, 1994), p. 12.

29. Paul E. Kelly, "Second Opinion," in *The Art and Politics of College Teaching: A Practical Guide for the Beginning Professor*, ed. R. McLaran Sawyer et al. (New York: Peter Lang, 1992), p. 285.

30. Kim A. McDonald, "Too Many Co-Authors?" *Chronicle of Higher Education*, Apr. 28, 1995, sec. A, p. 35.

31. Seldin (1993), p. 7.

32. Boyer, Altbach, and Whitelaw (1994), p. 49.

33. University of California, San Diego, "Report of the Task Force on Faculty Reward System," Oct. 1991, p. 9.

34. Ball State University, *A Different Dawn: A Proposal: Scholarship Reconsidered for Ball State University* (Muncie, Ind.: author), p. 10.

35. Richard C. Atkinson and Donald Tuzin, "Equilibrium in the Research University," *Change* (May/June 1992), p. 22.

Chapter Two

1. University of California, "Academic Personnel Manual" (Oakland, Calif., July 15, 1992), p. 4.

2. Lee S. Shulman, "Teaching as Community Property," *Change* (Nov./Dec. 1993), p. 6.

3. Thomas J. Schlereth, "Museum Exhibition Reviews," *Journal of American History* (June 1989), p. 192.

4. Shulman (1994), p. 6.

5. American Association for Higher Education, "From 'My Work' to 'Our Work': Realigning Faculty Work with College and University Purposes," Third AAHE Conference on Faculty Roles and Rewards, Phoenix, Ariz., Jan. 19–22, 1995.

6. Richard Chait, "The Future of Academic Tenure," *Priorities* (Washington, D.C.: Association of Governing Boards), no. 3 (Spring 1995).

7. Wayne C. Booth, *The Vocation of a Teacher: Rhetorical Occasions 1967–1988* (Chicago: University of Chicago Press, 1988), p. 320.

8. National Science Foundation, "Information for Reviewers," Washington, D.C.

9. American Chemical Society, report form for reviewers, *The Journal of Organic Chemistry* (Berkeley, Calif.).

10. University of California Press, confidential manuscript reading report (Berkeley, Calif.).

11. *American Journal of Sociology*, editor's form (Chicago, Ill.).

12. The Johns Hopkins University Press, letter of instruction from editors to readers of manuscripts (Baltimore, Md.).

13. American Chemical Society, "Instructions to Reviewers," *Environmental Science and Technology*, Washington, D.C.

14. University of Kentucky, "Policy for Faculty Performance Review" (Lexington, Ky., 1992), p. 4.

15. National Institute of Justice, "Criteria for Review of NIJ Proposals by Practitioner Reviewers" (Chicago, Ill.), p. 1.

16. Council of Graduate Schools, *The Doctor of Philosophy Degree: A Policy Statement* (Washington, D.C., 1990), p. 1.

17. Booth (1988), p. 212.

18. Malcolm M. MacDonald, director, University of Alabama Press, Tuscaloosa, Ala., letter to Mary Taylor Huber, Oct. 6, 1992.

19. University Press of New England, "Manuscript Evaluation Guidelines" (Hanover, N.H.).

20. The Charles Stewart Mott Foundation, *Philosophy Programs and Procedures,* (Flint, Mich., 1994), p. 15.

21. Lee S. Shulman, "Knowledge and Teaching: Foundations of the New Reform," *Harvard Educational Review* 57, no. 1 (Feb. 1987), p. 11; C. Wright Mills, *The Sociological Imagination* (London: Oxford University Press, 1959), p. 195; Donald A. Schön, *The Reflective Practitioner: How Professionals Think in Action* (London: Basic Books, 1983), p. 128.

22. Jacob Bronowski, *The Common Sense of Science* (Cambridge, Mass.: Harvard University Press, 1978), p. 99.

23. University of Iowa Press, "Instructions to Our Readers" (Iowa City, Iowa).

24. The American Physical Society, "Advice to Referees," *Physical Review Letters* (Ridge, N.Y.).

25. *Child Development,* "Consultant's Recommendation" (Chicago, Ill.).

26. Kansas State University, "Effective Faculty Evaluation: Annual Salary Adjustments, Tenure, and Promotion" (Manhattan, Kans., 1991).

27. Clemson University, "Questionnaire for Student Evaluation of Instructors" (Clemson, S.C.).

28. State University of New York, College at Old Westbury, "Manual for Reappointment, Promotion, and Tenure" (Old Westbury, N.Y., Fall 1981).

29. Edward Shils, *The Academic Ethic* (Chicago: University of Chicago Press, 1984), p. 10.

30. Mills (1959), p. 224.

31. University of Hawaii Press, "Guidelines for the Readers of Scholarly Manuscripts" (Honolulu, Hawaii).

32. University of Arizona Press, "Confidential Manuscript Appraisal" (Tucson, Ariz.).

33. The American Chemical Society, "Instructions to Reviewers," *The Journal of Physical Chemistry* (Los Angeles, Calif.).

34. University of Illinois at Urbana–Champaign, "A Faculty Guide for Relating Continuing Education and Public Service to the Promotion and Tenure Review Process," attachment III (Champaign, Ill., 1992–93), p. 2.

35. Richard Rhodes, *The Making of the Atomic Bomb* (New York: Simon and Schuster, 1988), p. 35.

36. Clifford Geertz, *Local Knowledge: Further Essays in Interpretive Anthropology* (New York: Basic Books, 1983), p. 157.

37. Oliver Sacks, "Prodigies," *New Yorker,* Jan. 9, 1995, p. 65.

38. Sidney I. Landau, editorial director, Cambridge University Press, North American Branch, New York, N.Y., letter to Mary Taylor Huber, Oct. 6, 1992.

39. University Press of Kansas, "Readers Report" (Lawrence, Kans.).

40. American Mathematical Society, "Information for Editors and Referees of Articles Submitted to the American Mathematical Society for Publication" (Providence, R.I.).

41. University Press, Kent State University, "Confidential Manuscript Reading Report" (Kent, Ohio), p. 1.

42. National Academy Press, "Guideline for the Review of National Research Council Reports" (Washington, D.C., July 1989).

43. Mott Foundation (1994), p. 15.

44. University of Georgia, "Guidelines for Appointment, Promotion, and Tenure" (Athens, Ga., May 7, 1992).

45. Parker J. Palmer, "Good Talk about Good Teaching," *Change* (Nov./Dec. 1993), p. 10.

46. Freeman J. Dyson, "Science in Trouble," *American Scholar* (Autumn 1993), p. 519.

47. Lee S. Shulman, "Teaching as Community Property," pp. 6–7.

48. Patricia Nelson Limerick, "Dancing with Professors: The Trouble with Academic Prose," *New York Times Book Review,* Oct. 31, 1993, sec. 7, p. 3.

49. Abraham Ibn Ezra, *Yeshod Mora (Fountain of the Knowledge of God, 1158),* as quoted in *A Teacher's Treasury of Quotations,* ed. Bernard E. Farber (Jefferson, N.C.: McFarland, 1985), p. 178.

50. Ralph Waldo Emerson, "The American Scholar: An Oration Delivered Before the *Phi Beta Kappa* Society at Cambridge, August 31, 1837," in *The Collected Works of Ralph Waldo Emerson, Volume I: Nature, Addresses, and Lectures,* ed. Robert E. Spiller and Alfred R. Ferguson (Cambridge, Mass.: Harvard University Press, 1971), p. 53.

51. Mills (1959).

52. Evelyn Fox Keller, *A Feeling for the Organism: The Life and Work of Barbara McClintock* (New York: Freeman, 1983), p. 206.

53. Ernest A. Lynton, *Making the Case for Professional Service* (Washington, D.C.: American Association for Higher Education, 1995), p. 25.

54. Schön (1983), p. 269.

Chapter Three

1. Russell Edgerton, Patricia Hutchings, and Kathleen Quinlan, *The Teaching Portfolio: Capturing the Scholarship in Teaching* (Washington, D.C.: American Association of Higher Education, 1991), p. 6.

2. Michael Bérubé, "Public Perceptions of Universities and Faculty," *Academe* (July/Aug. 1996), p. 17.

3. Kendrick A. Clements, "Promotion and Tenure for Public Historians," *Organization of American Historians Council of Chairs Newsletter* (Bloomington, Ind., Apr. 1988), p. 6.

4. Richard C. Gebhardt, "Avoiding the 'Research Versus Teaching' Trap: Expanding the Criteria for Evaluating Scholarship," in *The Politics and Processes of Scholarship,* ed. Joseph M. Moxley and Lagretta Lenker (Westport, Conn.: Greenwood Press, 1995), pp. 12–13.

5. University Task Force on Faculty Evaluation and the Executive Committee of the University Task Force on the Impact of Tenure and Promotion Practices upon Excellence at Kansas State University, *Effective Faculty Evaluation: Annual Salary Adjustments, Tenure, and Promotion: A Resource for Faculty and Administrators* (Manhattan, Kans., May 1992), p. 5.

6. Patricia Hutchings, introduction to *Campus Use of the Teaching Portfolio: Twenty-Five Profiles,* ed. Erin Anderson (Washington, D.C.: American Association for Higher Education, 1993); Edgerton, Hutchings, and Quinlan (1991); Peter Seldin and Associates, *Successful Use of Teaching Portfolios* (Bolton, Mass.: Anker, 1993).

7. Robert C. Froh, Peter J. Gray, and Leo M. Lambert, "Representing Faculty Work: The Professional Portfolio," in *Recognizing Faculty Work: Reward Systems for the Year 2000,* ed. Robert Diamond and Bronwyn E. Adam (San Francisco: Jossey-Bass, 1993), p. 100.

8. Edgerton, Hutchings, and Quinlan (1991), p. 8.

9. Russell Edgerton, "The Re-Examination of Faculty Priorities," *Change* (July/Aug. 1993), p. 20.

10. Northeastern University Strategic Planning Task Force on Faculty, Final Report (Boston, Mass., May 24, 1993), p. 7.

11. University of Kentucky, "Teaching Portfolio," *Administrative Regulations,* appendix I (Lexington, Ky., June 11, 1992), p. 4.

12. Rensselaer Polytechnic Institute, *Biographical Sketch and Professional Activities* (Troy, N.Y.), pp. 12–22.

13. Ernest A. Lynton, *Making the Case for Professional Service* (Washington, D.C.: American Association for Higher Education, 1995), pp. 22–23.

14. Edgerton, Hutchings, and Quinlan (1991), pp. 3–4.

15. Larry A. Braskamp and John C. Ory, *Assessing Faculty Work: Enhancing Individual and Institutional Performance* (San Francisco: Jossey-Bass, 1994), p. 112.

16. Kenneth Wolf, "Teaching Portfolios: Capturing the Complexities of Teaching," in *Valuing Teachers' Work: New Directions in Teacher Appraisal*, ed. Lawrence Ingvarson and Rod Chadbourne (Victoria: Australian Council for Educational Research, 1994), p. 128.

17. Ernest L. Boyer, Philip G. Altbach, and Mary Jean Whitelaw, *The Academic Profession: An International Perspective* (Princeton, N.J.: The Carnegie Foundation for the Advancement of Teaching, 1994), p. 86.

18. John A. Centra, *Reflective Faculty Evaluation: Enhancing Teaching and Determining Faculty Effectiveness* (San Francisco: Jossey-Bass, 1993), pp. 89–91.

19. Patricia Hutchings, "Peer Review of Teaching: 'From Idea to Prototype,'" *AAHE Bulletin* 47(3) (Nov. 1994), p. 2.

20. Steven G. Olswang, vice provost, University of Washington (Seattle), letter to Mary Taylor Huber, Mar. 9, 1994.

21. Duquesne University, *Promotion, Tenure, and/or Third-Year Review: Guidelines for Faculty and Administrators* (Pittsburgh, Penn., July 1991), p. 9.

22. Frederick Lovejoy, Jr., and Mary B. Clark, "A Promotion Ladder for Teachers at Harvard Medical School: Experience and Challenges," *Academic Medicine* 70(12) (Dec. 1995), pp. 1079–1086; Daniel Toteson, dean, Harvard Medical School, "Final Guidelines for Clinician Scholar Track," internal memorandum, Mar. 25, 1995.

Chapter Four

1. Northeastern University Strategic Planning Task Force on Faculty, "Final Report" (Boston, May 24, 1993), pp. 7–8.

2. Peter J. Gray, Robert M. Diamond, and Bronwyn E. Adam, *A National Study on the Relative Importance of Research and Undergraduate Teaching at Colleges and Universities* (Syracuse, N.Y.: Center for Instructional Development, Syracuse University, Feb. 1996), p. 62.

3. Alan E. Guskin, "Facing the Future: The Change Process in Restructuring Universities," *Change* (July/Aug. 1996), p. 34.

4. Associated New American Colleges, "An Educational Model for the Future: An Overview" (Chicago, 1996), p. 1.

5. Theodora J. Kalikow, interim president, Plymouth State College (Plymouth, N.H.), letter to Ernest L. Boyer, Sept. 4, 1992.

6. Judith B. Walzer, provost, New School for Social Research (New York), letter to Ernest L. Boyer, Sept. 30, 1992.

7. American Association of University Professors, "1940 Statement of Principles on Academic Freedom and Tenure: With 1970 Interpretive Comments," appendix to David A. Dilts et al., *Assessing What Professors Do: An Introduction to Academic Performance Appraisal in Higher Education* (Westport, Conn.: Greenwood Press, 1994), p. 115.

8. Max E. Pierson, "Who's Going to Evaluate Me and On What?" *School Administrator* 52(9) (Oct. 1995), p. 18.

9. Raoul A. Arreola, *Developing a Comprehensive Faculty Evaluation System* (Bolton, Mass.: Anker, 1995), p. 4.

10. Robert Boice, *The New Faculty Member: Supporting and Fostering Professional Development* (San Francisco: Jossey-Bass, 1992), p. 38.

11. Robert M. Diamond, *Serving on Promotion and Tenure Committees: A Faculty Guide* (Bolton, Mass.: Anker, 1994), pp. 5–7.

12. Russell Edgerton, Patricia Hutchings, and Kathleen Quinlan, *The Teaching Portfolio: Capturing the Scholarship in Teaching* (Washington, D.C.: American Association for Higher Education, 1991), p. 51.

13. George R. LaNoue and Barbara A. Lee, *Academics in Court: The Consequences of Faculty Discrimination Litigation* (Ann Arbor: University of Michigan Press, 1987), p. 83.

14. Northwestern University, "Teaching and the Faculty Reward System at Northwestern," attachment C (Evanston, Ill.), 1991.

15. Pennsylvania State University, "A Campaign for Excellence: The Report of the Task Force on Undergraduate Education" (University Park, Sept. 1991), p. 22.

16. University of California, Berkeley, "Report of the Universitywide Task Force on Faculty Rewards" (Oakland, Calif.), June 26, 1991, p. 1.

17. John A. Centra, *Reflective Faculty Evaluation: Enhancing Teaching and Determining Faculty Effectiveness* (San Francisco: Jossey-Bass, 1993), p. 166.

18. William P. Gallé, Jr., and Clifford M. Koen, Jr., "Tenure and Promotion after Penn *v. EEOC,*" *Academe* (Sept.–Oct. 1993), pp. 19–26.

19. Lorenzo Middleton, "Academic Freedom *vs.* Affirmative Action: Georgia Professor Jailed in Tenure Dispute," *Chronicle of Higher Education,* Sept. 2, 1980, p. 1.

20. Christopher Clausen, "Faculty Workloads and Legislative Curiosity," *Academe* 82(5) (Sept.–Oct. 1996), pp. 42–43.

21. American Association of University Professors, "Statement on Procedural Standards in the Renewal or Nonrenewal of Faculty Appointments, 1989," appendix to *Assessing What Professors Do: An Introduction to Academic Performance Appraisal in Higher Education,* by David A. Dilts, Laurence J. Haber, and Donna Bialik (Westport, Conn.: Greenwood Press, 1994), p. 125.

22. Robin Wilson, "Scheduling Motherhood," *Chronicle of Higher Education,* Mar. 10, 1995, pp. A14–A15.

Chapter Five

1. Carol S. Gruber, *Mars and Minerva: World War I and the Uses of Higher Learning in America* (Baton Rouge: Louisiana State University, 1975), pp. 198–199.

2. Ellen W. Schrecker, *No Ivory Tower: McCarthyism and the Universities* (New York: Oxford University Press, 1986).

3. Anne Draffkorn Kilmer, "On the Antiquity of Man's Commitment to Excellence in Scholarship," paper presented to the California Scholarship Federation, Millbrae, Calif., Apr. 20, 1985, p. 12.

4. *Oxford English Dictionary,* 9th edition, s.v. "scholar."

5. Ralph Waldo Emerson, "The American Scholar: An Oration Delivered Before the *Phi Beta Kappa* Society at Cambridge, August 31, 1837," in *The Collected Works of Ralph Waldo Emerson, Volume I: Nature, Addresses, and Lectures,* ed. Robert E. Spiller and Alfred R. Ferguson (Cambridge, Mass.: Harvard University Press, 1971) p. 61.

6. Emerson (1971), pp. 62–65.

7. Wayne C. Booth, *The Vocation of a Teacher: Rhetorical Occasions 1967–1988* (Chicago: University of Chicago Press, 1988), pp. 67–75.

8. Eric Ashby, "A Hippocratic Oath for the Academic Profession," *Minerva* 7(1–2) (1968–69), pp. 64–66.

9. American Association of University Professors, "Statement on Professional Ethics," *Academe* (July–Aug. 1987) p. 49.

10. Talcott Parsons, "The Academic System: A Sociologist's View," *Public Interest* 13 (Fall 1968), p. 186.

11. Edward Shils, *The Academic Ethic* (Chicago: University of Chicago Press, 1984), p. 62.

12. *The American Heritage Dictionary*, 2nd College Edition, s.v. "honesty."

13. National Academy of Sciences, *Responsible Science: Ensuring the Integrity of the Research Process, Volume I* (Washington, D.C.: author, 1992), pp. 5–6.

14. Confucius, *The Confucian Analects* (14/3), as quoted in John Bartlett, *Familiar Quotations*, 14th edition, ed. Emily Morison Beck (New York: Little, Brown, 1968), p. 72.

15. Shils (1984), p. 42.

16. American Historical Association, *Statements on Standards of Professional Conduct* (Washington, D.C.: author, 1993), p. 1.

17. Booth (1988), pp. 67–68.

18. American Historical Association (1993), p. 3.

19. Booth (1988), p. 329.

20. C. Wright Mills, "On Intellectual Craftsmanship," in *The Sociological Imagination* (New York: Oxford University Press, 1959), p. 196.

21. Louis J. Rubin, "Ralph W. Tyler: A Remembrance," *Phi Delta Kappan* 75(10) (June 1994), p. 784.

22. David L. Wheeler, "Scientists Explore How the Brain Improves the Body's Defenses Against Disease," *Chronicle of Higher Education*, Nov. 22, 1996, pp. A10–A11.

23. Thomas Ehrlich, *The Courage to Inquire: Ideals and Realities in Higher Education* (Bloomington: University of Indiana Press, 1995), p. 147.

24. Thomas Bender, *Intellect and Public Life: Essays on the Social History of Academic Intellectuals in the United States* (Baltimore: The Johns Hopkins University Press, 1993), p. 137.

25. The University of California, Berkeley, "Report of the Universitywide Task Force on Faculty Rewards" (Oakland, Calif., June 26, 1991), p. 16.

INDEX